MW01620308

Carmen Ohio

Oh come let's sing Ohio's praise
And songs to Alma Mater raise
While our hearts rebounding thrill
With joy which death alone can still
Summer's heat or winter's cold
The seasons pass the years will roll
Time and change will surely (truly) show
How firm thy friendship ... O-HI-O.

These jolly days of priceless worth
By far the gladdest days on earth
Soon will pass and we not know
How dearly we love O-HI-O!

We should strive to keep thy name
Of fair repute and spotless fame
So in college halls we'll grow
And love thee better ... O-HI-O!

Though age may dim our mem'ry's store
We'll think of happy days of yore
True to friend and frank to foe
As sturdy sons of O-HI-O
If on seas of care we roll
Neath blackened sky or barren shoal
Thoughts of thee bid darkness go
Dear Alma Mater...O-HI-O!!

Dwight Hudson, Ohio State Univerisity Marching Band drum major 1977-1979, provided much entertainment for Buckeye fans for three years, the longest term as drum major since "Tubby" Essington (OSUMB 1920-1922).

Dwight Hudson's showmanship and baton tricks amazed audiences. He first began twirling the baton in the sixth grade. During his tenure as drum major at Ohio State Hudson received many standing ovations.

ACKNOWLEDGEMENTS

THANKS

Our mission and vision for this book has been to document and preserve as much of the rich history and legacy of African-American students, alumni and others at The Ohio State University who have positively impacted our lives throughout the last 100 years. Since its founding in 1870 as a land-grant teaching and research university, the contributions made by African Americans at OSU have been inspirational.

The publisher is sincerely grateful for this exceptional opportunity to partner with the University in creating this unique work. We would like to acknowledge the dynamic leadership of OSU President E. Gordon Gee, who immediately embraced the idea of this work and assisted with the funding of this publishing project. Additionally, we would like to give thanks to the members of The Ohio State University Board of Trustees for their support of diversity initiatives at the University.

There were perhaps hundreds of others, too numerous to mention, who shared their stories and experiences as students while attending the University and for that we offer our thanks. Likewise, special thanks goes out to The Ohio State University community and departments who also supplied editorial content and historic photographs for this edition.

We are also proud to salute those African-American students, writers and photographers who have had an opportunity to showcase their talents and contributions to this historic book. We are appreciative to the many OSU alumni and friends like Bruce Wimbish, Debora Myles, Ron Ransom and Dickson Jenkins who have assisted us with this historic edition.

Special Assistant to the Publisher
Paula M. Gray

Executive Editor
Melanie Houston, '88

Senior Graphic Designer
Corey Favor

Graphic Designer
Jerrian Bell

Copy Editors
Nathan Wylder
Alisha C. Martin, '10

OSU Student Intern
Ababa Kifle

Years Of African-American Achievement At

Published in association with The Ohio State University

Ordering Information

Quantity Sales: Special discounts are available on quantity purchases by associations, corporations and others. For further details contact the publisher.

Corporate Headquarters:
1335 Dublin Road, Suite 50-A
Columbus, Ohio 43215
614-824-4154
www.CSunnyMartin.com

Photo Credits:
Ira Graham Photography
Terry Gilliam
The Ohio State University Archives, Photo Department

Printed in the United States of America

ISBN 10: 0615449778
ISBN 13: 978-0-615-44977-7

Ohio UNION
HOME
Ohio UNION
OHIO

Criteria for Inclusion

From ***Excellence to Eminence…100 Years of African-American Achievement at The Ohio State University*** presents an opportunity for us to document some of the rich history of African-American students, administrators and alumni at the University and afford them a measure of recognition for their career and civic achievements.

A sincere effort was made to include those OSU students, administrators and alumni whose accomplishments and achievements are significant, and whose contributions to their chosen careers and/or organizations, whether citywide, or on the national or global level have improved the quality of life for all of us.

In today's mobile society, no such publication could ever claim to be complete; some who should be included could not be reached or chose not to respond, and for that we offer our apologies. Constraints of time, space and awareness are thus responsible for other omissions, and not a lack of good intentions on the part of the publisher. Our goal was to document as much of the African-American history at The Ohio State University as possible.

An invitation to participate in the publication was extended solely at the discretion of the publisher. Biographies were invited to contribute personal and professional data, with only the information freely submitted to be included. The editors have made sincere efforts to present an accurate distillation of the data, and to catch errors whenever possible. However, the publisher cannot assume any responsibility for the accuracy of the information submitted.

There was no fee charged for inclusion in this publication and inclusion was not guaranteed. Comments and other concerns should be addressed to:

C. Sunny Martin
Managing Partner
C. Sunny Martin & Associates, LLC
1335 Dublin Rd, Suite 50-A
Columbus, Ohio 43215
614-824-4154
E-mail: sunny@csunnymartin.com
www.CSunnyMartin.com

Table of Contents

April, 2011

The members of The Ohio State University board of trustees extend greetings to our alumni and all readers of ***100 Years of African-American Achievement at The Ohio State University***. Recently, President E. Gordon Gee proudly remarked that the university has progressed from "good to great" and is well on its way to world-class eminence. We are confident in that future and know it couldn't be accomplished without the rich diversity of our OSU family.

Throughout our history, African Americans have strengthened OSU through their achievements in all walks of life, including the arts, education, business, athletics, community and military service, politics, science and much, much more. These individuals have added to the success and legacy of the university not only with their own achievements, but also through determination, endurance and devotion to the betterment of our community.

The incredible stories highlighted in this book are certain to inspire and educate all of us as we take our own personal journeys through life. It is one more reason I am honored to be affiliated with the university and to call OSU my alma mater. I extend my deepest appreciation to all who had a role in bringing this publication to life.

Sincerely,

Leslie H. Wexner
Chairman
The Ohio State University Board of Trustees

The Ohio State University Board of Trustees

Membership

Leslie H. Wexner
Chair
(2011)

Douglas G. Borror
Vice Chair
(2011)

Walden W. O'Dell
(2012)

Alex Shumate
(2012)

Brian K. Hicks
(2013)

John C. "Jack" Fisher
(2013)

Robert H. Schottenstein
(2014)

Alan W. Brass
(2014)

Ronald A. Ratner
(2015)

Algenon L. Marbley
(2016)

Linda S. Kass
(2017)

Janet B. Reid
(2018)

W. G. "Jerry" Jurgensen
(2018)

Jeffrey Wadsworth
(2019)

Clark G. Kellogg
(2019)

G. Gilbert Cloyd
Charter Trustee
(2012)

Alexis "Alex" L. Swain
Student Trustee
(2011)

Brandon N. Mitchell
Student Trustee
(2012)

FOREWORD

ROBERT M. DUNCAN

I was honored and humbled when C. Sunny Martin requested that I write the foreword for this historic publication, ***100 Years of African-American Achievement at The Ohio State University.***

Sunny was reared in Columbus, remains a resident and is thoroughly familiar with and affectionate towards the University. His late brother, United States Air Force Colonel George Martin, was a distinguished graduate of The Ohio State University College of Medicine. Unfortunately, Colonel Martin met an untimely death while on duty. So this publication regarding the University has special meaning to Sunny Martin.

Sunny's vision was to highlight the accomplishments of African Americans who attended the University. This work illustrates that he has stayed true to his vision. I gratefully applaud Sunny, his associates and the University for their efforts in publishing this work.

I came to Ohio State as a first-year student in 1945, just as World War II was ending. Graduating from the Moritz College of Law in 1952, it has been my good fortune to have been close to this great university for more than 65 years. Over the years, the University has manifested its continuing faith in the principles of its land-grant mission. I was, like many other African Americans with meager financial resources, first in my family to attend a truly great university and receive the life-long benefit of a "world class" higher education.

As this work clearly points out, Ohio State has a long history of providing African Americans with opportunities for education; however, like most American institutions, it has some history of unfortunate racial segregation.

When I came to Ohio State in 1945, there were no African Americans living on campus.

Most of us lived on the east side of Columbus and commuted to campus by streetcar. For the most part, our student activity was on the east side, where we received a high level of support from the African-American community.

Through the years, there has been a continuing presence of a strong African-American academic community at the University. After World War II, there were many black veterans who came to Ohio State with financial aid provided by the G.I. Bill of Rights. These veterans were mature, serious, worldly, studious and eager to become educationally armed to actively participate in social change. Their presence was extremely valuable, generally to the University and specifically to the African-American student community.

As a result of racial segregation there was a lack of opportunities in the South and numerous academically committed and gifted students migrated north to Ohio State and enrolled in graduate and professional programs. You will find some of them listed in this publication.

The African-American academic culture was strengthened by certain on-campus civic and social organizations. Black Greek letter organizations were a backbone of social and academic structural strength.

With retrospective appreciation, I recall the leadership role of Russell Jones, an administrator, who worked to enrich the campus life of black students.

At The Ohio State University, I, like many others, had the opportunity to come to know greatness. During my first month at the University, it was my great fortune to meet William "Deke" Willis. From that time on, I was honored to be one of his many personal friends. He was one of this country's greatest athletes – but an even greater human being.

This work chronicles the unequaled athletic and civic achievements of Jessie Owens. In 1948, Gloria Owens Hemphill was a student at Ohio State, and I was lucky to have become one of her many on-campus friends. Again, I as a member of the University community, I saw greatness by coming to know Jesse Owens and his wonderful family.

While an undergrad, I had some classes with my friends Dr. Samuel DuBois Cook and Clarence Clyde Ferguson, Esq. Both were top-of-the-class scholars. After graduation from Ohio State, Sam Cook became the first black professor at Duke University and president of Dillard University. Clyde Ferguson graduated from the Harvard Law School, served as dean of the Howard University Law School, taught at the Harvard Law School and was United States Ambassador to Uganda.

Ohio State experienced growth and change in the 1960s and 1970s.

We were fortunate to have campus activists and administrative leaders such as Vice Provost Frank Hale, who did much to design, lead and bring into reality a unique strategy to bring well qualified African-American students to Ohio State's graduate and professional programs.

From the 1980s and into the 21st century, we saw the fruits of increased diversity and inclusion efforts with a large influx of well qualified and talented African-American students, scholars, academic leaders and administrators. Alex Shumate was the first African-American chairman of the University board of trustees in 1997. I was honored to also serve as chair of the board in 2006-2007.

Time has passed and change has occurred, but the on-campus and extended Ohio State African-American community remains alive, well, socially and economically productive, ever improving and committed to the pursuit of excellence.

This publication provides illustrative insight into and recognition of the major role of The Ohio State University in bringing to reality the truth of our elders' admonition: get an education – once you get it – no one can take it away – and you will have a better day.

Robert M. Duncan

INTRODUCTION

E. GORDON GEE
PRESIDENT
THE OHIO STATE UNIVERSITY

Looking out from my office, I can see across the Oval, the very center of campus. I have found that if you spend enough time looking out those windows you will see most every student, faculty and staff member pass by on his or her way to class, to the library, or heading off toward the student union.

It is an inspiring view. What you see every day at The Ohio State University is a beautiful mosaic of people and cultures, and faces framed by promise and possibility.

Looking out on the Oval, or even studying the campus from the commanding views afforded in the reading room atop the Thompson Library, still cannot reveal the full picture and the depth of what takes place here.

The work, the mission and the people of this great university create an energy that radiates out from campus. Every person who comes to us in search of a better understanding of the world and a better grasp of his or her own potential leaves campus carrying this Ohio State experience with them in their careers and in their communities.

I think that is the essential message of this book. As you read, you will encounter the stories of African Americans, some world famous, some not terribly well known, but all celebrated products of an Ohio State education. Hope and triumph radiate from these pages and tell the story of a university that has helped move this state and nation toward its founding ideals of freedom and equality.

For many years, the NAACP magazine *The Crisis* ran an annual feature that served as something of a national census for African-American education in the United States. Near the end of World War I, *The Crisis* began surveying schools across the country and publishing a list of African-American high school graduates and African-American college students. Happily, in a few short years they were overwhelmed and had to adjust their plans. Instead of names, they began publishing only a count of students. It was a good problem to have. Indeed, as the editors noted in 1924, "We lose thus in personal touch but the results thus indicated are inspiring."

Looking back at *The Crisis* reports today, it is moving to see the central role Ohio State played in educating African Americans in an era when the doors to many colleges and universities were closed.

In that 1924 issue, *The Crisis* found that Ohio State had 225 African Americans enrolled. The group included men and women studying dentistry, electrical engineering, and all manner of other endeavors. Outside of historically black institutions, Ohio State was among the nation's leaders in African-American enrollment and in the number of degrees earned by African Americans.

By way of comparison, the next largest enrollment of African Americans in a Big Ten school was 78.

In the 1938 report, among all non-historically black institutions, Ohio State held the remarkable distinction of leading the nation in bachelor's degrees, master's degrees, and doctorates earned by African Americans.

Of the nine doctorates completed by African Americans in the nation that year, three were from Ohio State.

I have held those dissertations in my hands and it is a powerful experience. Between the frayed covers of those studies, typed on what are now yellowing pieces of paper, I read the work of scholars who undertook a most incredible journey to pursue their academic dreams. Yet, they not only persevered, they dedicated their work to helping others succeed.

One of those dissertations – by Joseph Himes – was a study of how African-American boys in Columbus could be set on a path toward success. Another – by Reid Jackson – considered how best to educate African Americans to thrive as teachers in the American South.

The power, not merely of their example but of their work, radiated from this campus and out into the world. With his doctorate in hand, Dr. Jackson went on to commit his life to education. He helped found Central State University in Ohio and taught at several colleges dedicated to providing opportunities to African Americans. Dr. Jackson was a fierce foe of segregation, organizing the Southern Negro Conference for Equalization of Education Opportunities to help make the case – years before the U.S. Supreme Court would endorse the view – that separate but equal was not only unequal but also unconscionable.

THE OHIO STATE UNIVERSITY · 1870 ·

Racism was not a theory to Dr. Himes or Dr. Jackson. It was not an experimental challenge to consider. It was reality in the lives of their subjects and in their own lives.

It pains me to admit this truth, but an honest account of Ohio State's great contributions toward the goal of equality must also acknowledge this university's shortcomings. At the time that Ohio State was leading the nation in providing educational opportunities to African Americans, this campus allowed racist practices to persist on what should have been the freest and fairest soil in the state.

The truly epic athletic accomplishments of Jesse Owens are well known to history and justly highlighted in this volume. One day in 1935, during his sophomore year at Ohio State, he stepped onto the track to compete in the conference championships. In the space of 45 minutes he broke three world records. And he tied another. It has been called the finest hour in the history of sports.

Only when you understand the reality of Jesse Owens' daily life can you even begin to appreciate the true measure of his astonishing accomplishments. Jesse Owens was a student unwelcome to live on his own campus, as the dormitories excluded African Americans. Jesse Owens was breaking world records without so much as winning a track scholarship. This son of sharecroppers and grandson of slaves had to work nights as an elevator operator to pay his tuition and afford the privilege of bringing great acclaim to the university. And this shining example of what an extraordinary student athlete is capable of accomplishing was not accepted into the campus honor society for student athletes.

Through every indignity, he endured. The power and grace and determination of Jesse Owens radiated out from this campus to the world, and then back again. Over time, Ohio State cast off the vestiges of racist and exclusionary policies and became an institution truly worthy of the ideals of freedom and equality, truly worthy to be the alma mater of Jesse Owens.

Today our goal is more than an open door. Instead, our mission is to create an environment where all of our students can thrive.

At the Todd Bell National Resource Center on the African American Male, for example, we have made the recruitment, retention and timely graduation of African-American men a priority. Applying the best research data available, the center seeks practical steps toward making campus a launching pad for African-American success.

Their work shows that one of the best ways to promote success inside the classroom is to promote connections between students outside the classroom. With a sense of community and connectedness, students are more likely to persist and succeed in their studies and more likely to collect a degree.

We have taken that lesson to heart and achieved startling results. During a recent five-year period, the overall university retention rate – measuring those freshmen who return to campus for their sophomore year – rose from 87.5 to 93.1 percent. Over the same five years, the African-American retention rate leapt from 78.1 to 91.6 percent. Among students who get a jump start on college life by taking part in the Bell Center's Early Arrival Program, the retention rate has averaged 95 percent.

The Bell Center is named after the late Todd Bell, whose path led him from Ohio State to professional football and back to Ohio State. He worked tirelessly on campus and in the community to ensure that students could find hope within themselves. The power of Todd Bell's vision still radiates in the center, across the campus, and beyond.

A brief word about a personal hero. Robert Duncan is a hero of The Ohio State University, and a hero of mine, because he is a man of vast ability and ceaseless devotion to his community and his university.

Throughout his life, Bob Duncan has been a first. On four different courts – including the Supreme Court of Ohio – he was the first African American to serve. Every barrier he broke only reinforced his resolve to see others live a life of fairness and freedom.

One of the major court battles Judge Duncan presided over was a school segregation case in Columbus. Though segregated education had been officially forbidden for many years, numerous school districts in the 1970s failed to live up to the spirit of the law. Judge Duncan's decision knocked down the doors of exclusion in Columbus schools and gave students the advantage of a school system built for equality. It was the kind of decision that changed lives. A judge who learned the law at Ohio State sent hope radiating from campus once again.

Today, we are proud to enroll more African-American students than at any time in The Ohio State University's history. That fact is a tribute to everything this university stands for and a tribute to everyone – including the men and women profiled in this book – who has helped make Ohio State the university of the American future.

E. Gordon Gee
President
The Ohio State University

Photo courtesy of Ira Graham

Archie Griffin
Ohio State Sr. V.P. for Alumni Relations
Alumni Association President/CEO

Greetings Alumni and Friends:

For many years, I have enjoyed reading many of the books published by C. Sunny Martin. I've found the stories in these publications both compelling and inspiring. They share examples of outstanding achievement and provide our young people with a wonderful look at African Americans who have excelled in many areas of expertise.

With this background in mind, I was thrilled when I first heard Sunny was focusing the lens on the university I love with "From Excellence to Eminence... 100 Years of African American Achievement at The Ohio State University." Our university has graduated many accomplished African Americans from Leon Ransom and Jesse Owens, to Judge Robert M. Duncan, Clotilde Bowen, Stephanie Hightower and U.S. Congresswoman Marcia Fudge. This university has a long and storied history of African American achievement. However, many of these stories have been largely untold, and I am thrilled to see them brought to light.

As Senior Vice President for Alumni Relations / President and CEO of the Ohio State University Alumni Association, I know that it is crucial to make certain that great stories about Ohio State alumni and friends have a platform. These stories always do a great job of connecting the past to the present and there is no better way to illustrate Ohio's State's rich history than by highlighting the people who have made our university so very special.

I hope you will find inspiration in these stories just as I have.

Sincerely,

Archie Griffin
Senior Vice President for Alumni Relations
Ohio State Alumni Association President/CEO

Stay Connected. *Make Ohio State Stronger.*™

Inclusion
makes us stronger.
Congratulations
to The Ohio
State University
for recognizing 100 years of African
American Achievement at the university
and in our communities. Thank you
for leveraging similarities and valuing
differences in the past, present and future.
Limitedbrands
VICTORIA'S SECRET / BATH & BODY WORKS / PINK / LA SENZA
HENRI BENDEL / WHITE BARN CANDLE CO. / C.O. BIGELOW

PETER H. CLARK

OSU'S FIRST AFRICAN-AMERICAN BOARD MEMBER, 1884

By Jessica A. Johnson, Ph.D. 

Peter Humphries Clark, a renowned public school educator, intellectual and political activist in Cincinnati, Ohio, during the mid to late 19th century, was the first African American appointed to The Ohio State University's board of trustees by Governor George Hoadly. Clark was selected after Hoadly, a Democrat, won Ohio's 1883 gubernatorial race over Republican challenger Joseph Foraker. Clark was one of several influential black leaders assigned to prominent positions by Hoadly, who had promised black Ohioans that he and the Democratic Party would not ignore their concerns for social uplift. Clark was particularly insightful regarding his involvement in Ohio's politics. He encouraged his constituents to meticulously examine both major parties and make them work for the black vote.

Prior to joining the Democrats, Clark, like most African Americans during this era, was a Republican. He supported Republican Rutherford B. Hayes in the 1876 presidential election and stumped for the party during the 1868 and 1872 campaigns. Clark then surprisingly joined the Workingmen's Socialist Party in 1877. This was an audacious move on his part as most well-known African- American leaders, including his close associate Frederick Douglass, remained loyal to the Republicans even though they did not deliver on their promises of reform for blacks in the South during Reconstruction. However, like Douglass, Clark remained heavily focused on civil rights issues, pushing for the enforcement of the 14th and 15th Amendments, and fighting for class and educational equality.

In many ways, Clark was a political maverick as he shifted his party alliances. He ran for Ohio Commissioner of Education on the Socialist ticket in 1877 and that same year gave a rousing, as well as controversial, speech to workers who were part of the Great Railroad Strike. Clark's espousal of socialist economic theory was the major theme of his address as he discussed the poverty of the working class. "The poor man's lot is at best a hard one," Clark fervently stated to the crowd. "His hand to hand struggle with the wolf of poverty leaves him no leisure for any of the amenities of life, his utmost rewards are a scanty supply for food, scanty clothing, scanty shelter, and if perchance he escapes a pauper's grave [he] is fortunate" *(The Cincinnati Commercial)*.

Clark went on to contend that the "evil of poverty" would be curable only if the government had sole control of capital, a position that few black leaders would have taken. Yet he firmly believed that wealth should not be in the hands of a select few but that all should benefit from the economic prosperity of the nation. At the end of his remarks Clark reminded the strikers of their electoral power, telling them that they held the "all compelling ballot" in their hands.

Although his socialist platform was not popular, Clark was able to successfully combine his political activism with his career in public education, and he had compiled an impressive resume before becoming a trustee of Ohio State. In the early 1850s, Clark published a weekly abolitionist newspaper, the *Herald of Freedom*, and he was the first teacher to be hired by Cincinnati black public schools. He later founded and became principal of John I. Gaines High School in 1866, Ohio's first public high school for blacks.

Clark viewed the role of education in the black community from a progressive perspective, and during this period Cincinnati was considered a "borderland" city that had the potential for black economic empowerment. Clark believed that education was the key to establishing financial stability and one of the primary academic objectives of Gaines was to prepare students for better jobs. Under Clark's leadership, Gaines became known for producing outstanding students who went on to become teachers, and graduates slowly began to form a small black middle class. Gaines thrived as a leading school for blacks in Cincinnati for two decades but was abruptly closed in 1889 by the Board of Education. Five years earlier Clark had opposed a mixed race schools law because black instructors would not be allowed to teach white children. Although the law did not pass, Clark was dismissed from his position.

Clark left Cincinnati several years after the closing of Gaines but continued to work in public schools. He retired in 1908 after teaching in Sumner High, a segregated school in St. Louis, Missouri. Historians credit Clark with being the nation's primary black public school educator due to his pioneering accomplishments in Ohio. It is fitting that he spent a small part of his exceptional career at Ohio State, an institution that would eventually offer African Americans opportunities for the social and economic advancement he envisioned.

References

The Cincinnati Commercial. 23 July 1877. Print.

Herz, Walter. "Peter H. Clark." *Unitarian Universalist Historical Society*. 1999-2011. Print.

"His hand to hand struggle with the wolf of poverty leaves him no leisure for any of the amenities of life..."

Robert S. Dorsey

Left: Woody Hayes, Jessie Owens, Robert Dorsey

The Ohio State University's willingness to invest in the education of Robert Sherwood Dorsey has reaped benefits that will affect generations.

Born in the "chocolate bayou" of Lafayette, Louisiana, in 1923, Dorsey rose to the top of the academic ladder despite the separate but unequal education in the South, graduating valedictorian of his 1941 Phillis Wheatley High School class in Houston, Texas.

College bound, his career was nearly cut short in 1944 when he was activated into the Army Specialized Training Program at Howard University and then shipped out with the Second Army to Germany with a new combat engineering battalion as a water purification specialist.

After an honorable discharge in 1946, Dorsey wanted to pursue his new found interest in engineering but no major university would accept him because of his color. At first glance, even The Ohio State University rejected him saying its first preference was to GIs in their home state, but Dorsey persisted in writing a personal letter to the registrar explaining that his home state of Texas would not accept him because of his color and by the way…he played football.

So, as the first black Ohio State University athlete to major in engineering in 1947, Dorsey became an academic all-star. And although he played as a tight end (# 83) with the famed Rose Bowl Team of 1949, it was his engineering statistics that got him recognized. He was the first black to be inducted into the engineering honorary fraternity Tau Beta Pi and the first black to be inducted in the mechanical engineering honorary fraternity, Pi Tau Sigma, a brand new major at the time. After graduation in 1949, Dorsey became one of the first black engineers in the nation to be hired by the General Electric Aircraft Division where he retired after 38 years of service. He went on to serve many years as a consultant to General Electric after retirement.

Dorsey never forgot his Ohio State University. After returning to GE's Evendale plant in Cincinnati, Ohio, in the 1950s, Dorsey was tapped by legendary Head Coach Woody Hayes to serve as a role model to the young athletes Hayes was recruiting. Thus began a close friendship that lasted for decades not only with Coach Hayes but the many football players and coaches that came after him including current Head Coach Jim Tressel.

Left: Robert Dorsey and daughters Jocelyn and Robin

His most prized photo that hangs in his personal "hall of fame" is with Coach Hayes and Olympic Gold Medalist Jesse Owens, a man he greatly admired.

Although Coach Hayes would never admit it, it was not an accident that Dorsey received the Distinguished Alumni Award from the NCAA along with Navy Secretary Bo Callaway after serving on a special NCAA task force. Nor was it an accident that Dorsey served as one of the first black members of The Ohio State University's board of trustees during the turbulent civil rights struggle where Ohio State was spared the negative publicity that rocked many campuses during that era.

Dorsey also served as the first black national president of the Ohio State Alumni Association and helped raise millions of dollars for his beloved alma mater. In fact there is a terrace which bears his name at the Longaberger Alumni House.

If you ask Dorsey what would be his biggest achievement in connection with the University next to marrying his Ohio State college sweetheart Helena Harris, an honor graduate in education, Dorsey would tell you sending the second generation to his alma mater was his crowning glory.

His three daughters attended Ohio State and are successful professionals. His oldest is an award-winning journalist and the first African-American anchor in a major television market in the South; his second daughter, a graduate of The Ohio State School of Veterinary Medicine is practicing in Cincinnati, Ohio; and his third daughter is a graphic design manager in Naples, Florida, and a graduate of The Ohio State School of Architecture and Industrial Design.

And if you have attended an Ohio State University football game, chances are you just might have seen Dorsey peering out of the University Suite onto the 50 yard line shouting, "Go Bucks!"

1947-48 OHIO STATE BUCKEYES

Wesley E. Fesler, Coach

ROBERT M. DUNCAN

By Jessica A. Johnson, Ph.D. 

As a young man from Urbana, Ohio, striving to shape his path in life during the late 1940s, Robert M. Duncan learned that discovering one's destiny takes time. While an undergraduate at The Ohio State University, Duncan had aspirations of becoming a teacher, and upon completion of his degree in secondary education he hoped to land a position at Champion Avenue Junior High School. The waiting list, however, was much longer than Duncan anticipated so he considered an offer to teach in Louisiana and even had a stint as a bellhop in Chicago. After much soul searching, Duncan finally decided to return to Ohio State and enroll in law school in 1949. Although the country was just a few years removed from World War II, OSU's academic community included zealous, young African-American students.

Duncan proved himself a scholar and leader at Ohio State, serving as president of his law class. Yet after his graduation in 1952, there were few opportunities for blacks in Ohio to practice law due to the majority of the profession being segregated. Most blacks worked in public jobs rather than private law firms. Duncan began to break down barriers by opening an office for the general practice of law in Columbus in 1954. Just three years later he became assistant attorney general of Ohio. Duncan would continue to advance his career in local and state government, holding the positions of attorney examiner for the Bureau of Workers' Compensation and assistant city attorney of Columbus. In 1966 he became judge of the Franklin County Municipal Court and the following year was elected to a full term. Governor James A. Rhodes appointed Duncan to Ohio's Supreme Court in 1969, making Duncan the first African American, and at that time the youngest, justice on the bench.

After serving two years on Ohio's Supreme Court, Duncan became the first African-American member of the U.S. Court of Military Appeals. He would later serve as judge of the United States District Court for the Southern District of Ohio, a position he held for 11 years. During his tenure on the federal bench, he wrote the historic order ending segregation in Columbus' public schools.

Duncan returned to private practice in 1985 with the Jones, Day, Reaves and Pogue law firm in Columbus after resigning from the judiciary. His alma mater beckoned in 1992, and Duncan was appointed vice president and general counsel to The Ohio State University. He also served a nine-year term on OSU's board of trustees, which included the position of chair from 2006 to 2007. Duncan has devoted his time and energy to Ohio State with the same fervor he had as a law student more than 50 years ago. Due to his influence on the campus and the lives of numerous law students, The Moritz College of Law honored Duncan with the William K. Thomas Distinguished Jurist Award at the Spring Hooding on May 9, 2008. Reflecting on his sterling career, Duncan is extremely modest about his accomplishments and credits much of his success to a simple attribute: courteousness.

"I've learned that manners will take you places where money won't," he says. "You must respect yourself, respect others and respect the space in which we all live."

Ohio UNION
Lead
LeadLearnServe.osu.edu
STATION 88
UniPrint
NOW OPEN!
ALL-IN-ONE

FOR MORE THAN 80 YEARS, NATIONWIDE HAS BEEN COMMITTED TO MAKING A DIFFERENCE IN THE COMMUNITIES WE SERVE. OUR PARTNERSHIP WITH THE OHIO STATE UNIVERSITY IS PART OF OUR HISTORY.

Nationwide®

As a Fortune 150 company headquartered in Columbus, we understand the importance of supporting our hometown institutions. We salute The Ohio State University and celebrate with them on this 100th year of African American achievement at The Ohio State University. It's especially fitting to honor one of the greatest athletes the world has known, the late Jesse Owens on this 75th year of his great Olympic Achievement.

Nationwide has one of the most diverse board of directors in the insurance industry. We believe our commitment to diversity and inclusion helps us fulfill our *On Your Side®* promise to the community, our customers, agents and associates, every day. We have many agents and associates who are proud OSU alumni and stand with the Buckeyes during this 100-year recognition.

We are proud of our associates and agents and their commitment to making a difference in our communities.

Nationwide helps to create opportunities for associates to engage in one of 34 associate business councils (ABCs) or associate resource groups (ARGs). These groups bring associates together around shared interests, help grow the business and help associates grow in leadership and career development. Several of our ARGs have formed alliances with OSU's student groups and the business school to help in recruiting and retaining talent.

Likewise, we are proud sponsors of OSU athletics – football, basketball and more. Our partnership with the university extends beyond our sponsorship of the sports teams.

NATIONWIDE IN THE COMMUNITY

LIMITED LISTING

The United Way
National Minority Supplier Diversity Council
The American Red Cross
The Central Intercollegiate Athletic Association (CIAA)
Historically Black Colleges and Universities (HBCUs)
Feeding America
The Smiley Group (Nationwide Insurance On Your Side® Tour with Tavis Smiley, PBS, TavisTalks.com)
Nationwide Children's Hospital
National Council of La Raza
NASCAR
National Black MBA Association
National Society of Hispanic MBA
National Urban League, (I Am Empowered)
NAACP
The Human Rights Campaign
National Council of Negro Women
The Memorial Tournament

In The Beginning...

By Ann Wagner Hill, Ph.D. 

We are not makers of history. We are made by history.
-Martin Luther King, Jr.

The contents of this book spring from countless hours of research and dedication to explore and present an overview of the experiences, challenges and achievements of African Americans at The Ohio State University. Although it is not presented as a comprehensive historical document, it is a tribute to those who have paved the way for African-American students at the University.

Historically, education for African Americans has been the guiding post for advancement in American society. African-American children were always reminded that the pursuit of a college degree was the ultimate goal and nothing less. This seemed to be the only road of achieving the American dream.

In 1862, Vermont Senator Justin Morrill sponsored the Morrill Land Grant Act. This law gave federal land to states for public colleges and universities. Prior to this Act, African Americans were excluded from attending these institutions of higher learning; however, the provisions of the amended Morrill Land Grant Act of 1890 stated that federal land-grant funds must be provided equally for both African-American and white students. This law would open many doors as African Americans would now seek to obtain that much sought-after degree in higher education.

Despite the forces of a segregated society, The Ohio State University admitted its first African-American student, Fred D. Patterson, in 1882, and by 1892 the first African-American male, Sherman Hamlin Guss, graduated with a liberal arts degree. By 1905, the first African-American female, Jessica Frances Stephens, received a Bachelor of Arts degree. As a result of these accomplishments, the seeds had been planted. New horizons, innovations, creativity and academic scholarship became the benchmarks for African-American achievements. Other noted OSU graduates would include Ruth Ella Moore, the first African American to earn a Ph.D., in 1933, and Clotilde Dent Bowen, the first African-American woman to graduate from The Ohio State University School of Medicine, in 1947. These efforts were indeed revolutionary.

With seemingly inclusiveness, African Americans still represented only a fraction of the student population. The ultimate aim of African Americans was to obtain educational equality. The perseverance can be seen in the life story of Peter Humphries Clark, the first African-American teacher in the Cincinnati black public schools. Mr. Clark was an abolitionist, a prominent national figure and assistant to Frederick Douglass; yet despite the climate of the time, Clark also became the first African-American board trustee of The Ohio State University in 1884.

The resilience of the African-American student population would set the stage for their generations and those that followed. African Americans such as Leon Ransom, a 1927 graduate of The Ohio State University College of Law, became a professor at Howard University and joined the NAACP legal team in 1930. Ransom, along with Thurgood Marshall, litigated the infamous *Brown v. the Board of Education* decision.

Although it took nearly 100 years, in 1957, George David Boston became the first tenured African-American professor followed by Olivia Bozeman in 1960.

The list of outstanding African-American scholars has continued the legacy of excellence in all fields of study. It has become increasingly clear that African Americans have made tremendous strides at The Ohio State University; yet there is much more that can and will be done.

The "separate but equal" doctrine was practiced at OSU, but the 1954 Supreme Court case reversed it, and provided optimism and hope for all African Americans, including the University community. These fundamental issues of equality through integration and education would lead the University to the establishment of the Black Studies Department in 1969. Further evidence of activism to mobilize the African-American students surfaced when the first annual convention of the National Council for Black Studies was held in 1977.

Despite inescapable racial tension and the limited boundaries which had created second-class citizenship for African Americans during the early years, The Ohio State University would see an increased enrollment of African Americans to approximately 4,000 students by 2010. Determined to enhance the quality of the educational experience for African Americans, the University vehemently constructed a blueprint which has led to the University's emergence as one of the country's premier institutions for African-American enrollment and retention.

Ruth Ella Moore
OSU's first Black Ph.D., 1933

The University has reaffirmed its commitment to equality for all students by establishing such initiatives as the Office of Minority Affairs; the Frank W. Hale, Jr. Black Cultural Center; the African American and African Studies Community Extension Center; the Todd Anthony Bell National Resource Center; and the Moritz College of Law Minority Outreach Program. By implementing the Renewing the Covenant: Diversity Objective and Strategies for 2007-2012, the University is determined to provide a more positive and constructive learning environment for all students.

Numerous strides have been made by such African-American graduates including: Keith Alford, associate professor, Syracuse University; Alonzo J. Bowling, assistant professor, The Ohio State University; Derrick Butler, engineer for Procter & Gamble; David Carter, Chancellor of the Connecticut State University system; Samuel D. Cook, former president of Dillard University; Charity A. Earley, first African American to be commissioned as an officer in the Woman's Auxiliary Corps; Charles Lyons Jr., former chancellor at Fayetteville State University; Henry Ponder, former president of Fisk University and president and CEO of the National Association for Equality Opportunity; Earl E. Thorp, past president of the Association for the Study of Afro-American Life and History; Charles Ross, associate professor at the University of Mississippi; and Barbara J. Warren, associate clinical professor in The Ohio State College of Nursing.

Laudable accomplishments have been made, but not without hardships and struggles. Perhaps the paradox of the "then and now" is the persistence of African-American students and the University's commitment to diversity and inclusion. This book has attempted to describe a partial journey and evolution of African Americans at The Ohio State University and will hopefully provide a measure of recognition and appreciation for the contributions of African Americans to the growth, acclaim and prestige of The Ohio State University.

FROM EXCELLENCE TO EMINENCE

Office of Diversity and Inclusion

102 Bricker Hall
190 North Oval Mall
Columbus OH 43210-1358
Phone 614-292-4355
Fax 614-292-0224

Greetings:

This volume, *From Excellence to Eminence: 100 Years of African American Achievement at The Ohio State University*, coincides with the 40th anniversary of the Office of Diversity and Inclusion. Since our beginnings as the Office of Minority Affairs, we have served the university community by providing forty years of scholarship awards and services, pipeline projects, recruitment activities, and academic advancement services.

As an administrative unit, we remain committed to advancing academic excellence by increasing and advocating for campus diversity, inclusion and access. The Office continues to undertake initiatives aimed at these goals. It has been the duty and passion of this office to support the academic and professional advancement of underrepresented groups at Ohio State. For this reason, it is our honor to contribute to a volume that does much to showcase and celebrate the legacy of African American achievement at The Ohio State University.

Since its inception, our office has understood true education and diversity to be inseparable, interdependent and inextricable. For African Americans, education has always been a pathway to freedom. As Harlem Renaissance poet Langston Hughes has said, "[we] dream a world where all / Will know sweet freedom's way." Education is a sweet freedom.

Sincerely,

Valerie B. Lee

Valerie B. Lee
Vice Provost and
Chief Diversity Officer

ORIGINS AND SERVICES

It was during the turbulent campus crises of 1968 and the many months following the assassination of Dr. Martin Luther King Jr. that African-American students at The Ohio State University confronted the university administration with a set of demands. They called for the hiring of more African-American faculty and senior level administrative personnel; the establishment of a Black Cultural Center; the recruitment of African-American students; the establishment of a Department of African-American Studies; more student employment opportunities; more funds for African-American programming and publication; and lower student fees.

Times for these students were laced with struggle and determination. In response, Ohio State created the Office of Minority Affairs (OMA) during the 1969-1970 academic year, with Dr. William J. Holloway serving as its first Vice Provost from 1970 to 1978.

Now known as the Office of Diversity and Inclusion (ODI), the unit was initially created to recruit African-American students to Ohio State. However, under the guidance of Vice Provosts and Administrative Heads who represent some of the best in African-American leadership in higher education, the unit's scope expanded significantly, and in the academic year 2010-2011 the unit celebrated forty years of service as a(n): advisor to students and administration; coordinator and disseminator of information; sponsor of special programs and activities; and most importantly, an advocate for all historically underrepresented students, faculty and staff throughout the university.

Dr. William Jimmerson Holloway
Vice Provost, 1970-1978

Dr. Frank Hale Jr.
Vice Provost, 1978-1988

Ms. Linda Jackson
Interim Vice Provost, 1988-1989
Dr. Joseph Russell
Vice Provost, 1989-1992

David Williams II, Esq.
Interim Vice Provost, 1992-1993

Leroy Pernell, Esq.
Vice Provost, 1994-1997

Ms. Barbara Rich
Interim Vice Provost, 1997-1999

Dr. Timothy Knowles
Vice Provost, 1999-2000

Dr. Mac A. Stewart
Vice Provost, 2000-2010

Dr. Valerie B. Lee
Vice Provost, 2010-Present

In keeping with the motto, "Excellence through Diversity," the Office of Diversity and Inclusion offers a comprehensive body of services that range from scholarship support to pipeline programming, from retention services to cultural activities for faculty, staff and students.

For many students from underrepresented groups at Ohio State, their success begins with a scholarship from the Freshman Foundation Program (FFP) or Morrill Scholars Program (MSP). FFP began in the inaugural year of OMA, 1970-1971, to provide need-based support for Ohio students throughout their undergraduate years and is still providing students with aid today. MSP is Ohio State's premier diversity/merit scholarship program that actively recruits the country's most academically talented high school seniors from underrepresented groups. Since it began in 1983 with a modest forty students, the MSP has grown to be Ohio State's principal diversity contributor by annually providing over forty full tuition scholarships to incoming freshmen and regularly developing new recruitment pipelines throughout the United States in order to reach communities that will continue to enhance Ohio State's diversity. In addition to creating educational opportunities for undergraduate students, FFP and MSP also function as educational tools for the Ohio State academic community by creating a critical mass of student scholars who serve as true role models at the university and infuse all of Ohio State's academic programs with representation from underrepresented groups.

As part of efforts to develop talented high school students, in 1988 ODI developed the highly successful pre-collegiate pipeline program, the Young Scholars Program (YSP). YSP is a unique venture between Ohio State and Ohio urban school districts in cities across the state. The program identifies and serves high-achieving first-generation students from economically challenged backgrounds in order to increase the presence of academic students seeking college degrees at Ohio State.

YSP Scholars, 2007

The Office also maintains one of the oldest graduate pipeline programs for underrepresented groups. The Graduate and Professional Schools Visitation Days (GPSVD) has been serving Ohio State for forty years. The GPSVD was instituted in the The Office also maintains one of the oldest graduate pipeline programs for underrepresented groups. The Graduate and Professional Schools Visitation Days (GPSVD) has been serving Ohio State for forty years. The GPSVD was instituted in the autumn of 1971 under the direction of Dr. Frank W. Hale Jr., who was appointed Associate Dean of the Graduate School that summer and Vice Provost of Minority Affairs in 1978. In the autumn of 1978, the sponsorship of GPS was transferred to the Office of Minority Affairs.

Since its early years, GPSVD has expanded to a campus visit that connects more than forty academic departments with students from more than forty colleges and universities. During their visit to Ohio State, undergraduate scholars meet with faculty and administrative liaisons from Ohio State academic units and speak with current graduate and professional students about advanced study at Ohio State.

A panel of graduate and professional students responds to questions from visiting undergraduate scholars.

Visiting undergraduate scholars receive information about funding opportunities at Ohio State.

GPS organizer and Director of Special Programs, Ms. Rose Wilson-Hill comments, "GPS has been a cross-collaboration between the Office of Diversity and Inclusion, the Graduate School, the Professional Colleges and a host of colleges and universities across the country (and more recently, Puerto Rico) for forty years and has changed the lives of hundreds of students from historically black colleges and universities, Hispanic-serving institutions, and predominately white institutions who may not otherwise have known of the opportunity to come to Ohio State to complete their post-baccalaureate degrees. As they continue to contribute to their chosen fields of preparation, they are forever embedded in the fabric of what helps to make Ohio State great."

Ms. Rose Wilson-Hill welcomes students on the first night of the annual GPSVD event.

Another signature program is ACCESS Collaborative. Created in 1989, ACCESS works to increase retention and graduation rates of low-income single parent students. The program coordinates university and community support services to meet low-income single parents' needs as students and as heads of household. Students receive academic support such as advising and tutoring; parenting skills addressing child development and nutrition; financial literacy; life skills; stress management and career development.

Student-parents at ACCESS orientation

One of the most important features of the Office of Diversity and Inclusion is its emphasis on retention. Through the unit's efforts, scholars stay informed about financial aid procedures to retain their student financial aid. The unit's professionals provide tutoring, mentoring and advising services to assist them in reaching their full academic potential and map their undergraduate career path in ways that are most preparatory for their post-baccalaureate goals.

The Office of Diversity and Inclusion is also headquarters to two nationally recognized centers: the Frank W. Hale, Jr. Black Cultural Center (Hale Center) and the Todd Bell

A tutor in our Academic Advancement Services helps students during an end-of-the-quarter review session.

National Resource Center for the African American Male (BRC).

Under the direction of Mr. Larry Williams, the Hale Center has become one of the finest black cultural centers in the country and celebrates the contributions of African Americans in the world of arts, letters and science. It is recognized by the Association of Black Cultural Centers (ABCC) as a national model for similar culturally relevant facilities and ranked within the top 10 Black Cultural Centers in the country. Open 86 hours a week within a seven-day schedule, the Center provides numerous opportunities for the entire university and Columbus community. The Center distinguishes itself from other centers with its large and outstanding art collection, two computer labs, and academic and educational classes offered through art education, African American and African studies,

Larry Williamson, Director, Frank W. Hale, Jr. Black Cultural Center

women's studies, social work, English, history, music and dance. It is host to cultural, social and educational programs and workshops for the entire university and, in fact, is one of the few centers that has an official academic and cultural component within the structure of the building. At any given time, the Hale Center holds one-sixth to one-fourth of the activities for African-American students on campus; it holds 25 to 40 percent of the programs available during Black History Month. For an in-depth history of the Hale Center, read Dr. Hale's "The History of the Frank W. Hale Black Cultural Center at The Ohio State University" in this volume.

Students listen to keynote speakers at the BRC's annual Gathering of Men event.

The Todd Anthony Bell National Resource Center on the African American Male is dedicated to addressing the broad range of critical issues facing black men. The Center was established in 2005 in response to national and local research studies about the performance of African-American male students in college; this research inspired administrators at The Ohio State University, particularly former Vice Provost Mac Stewart, to implement a pilot effort to better understand and improve retention and graduation rates for these students.

BRC Director Dr. James Moore, III and Program Director Mr. Todd Suddeth pictured with high-achieving African-American students at the BRC's annual Recognition Ceremony

Research led the Office of Diversity and Inclusion, the Office of Student Affairs, and a host of other faculty and staff members at Ohio State to establish the Black Male Initiative under the leadership of Mr. Todd Bell, Ohio State alumnus and retired NFL football player. The emergence of the Black Male Initiative led to significant improvements in student satisfaction, performance and retention to graduation.

So that the campus as a whole might benefit from the lessons learned through the Black Male Initiative, the Office of Diversity and Inclusion established an on-campus center to continue and expand the efforts of the Black Male Initiative. The Todd Anthony Bell National Resource Center on the African American Male (BRC), named posthumously after Todd Bell, was approved in 2004 and opened in September of 2005.

Since its inception, the center has prioritized the production of robust research studies that inform social policy and theory on African-American males and developed research-based programs, models and initiatives that can be replicated at other institutions.

Under the leadership of Dr. James Moore, III (Director) and Todd Suddeth (Program Director), the BRC has thrived, having successfully created a sense of community and connectedness among African-American men at Ohio State to ensure their success in college and beyond.

Todd Suddeth, Program Director, Todd Bell National Resource Center for the African American Male

BRC initiatives such as the Early Arrival Program, which teaches students about strategies and resources to help with academic achievement and helps develop their professional and leadership skills, have played a pivotal role in student success. As Suddeth notes, "The Todd A. Bell National Resource Center is the most comprehensive organization in the United States in facilitating success for African-American male college students. The Ohio State University's Office of Diversity and Inclusion has taken the initiative in developing a national model to foster academic achievement and overall development with this population."

The BRC expects to serve as a national resource for those individuals interested in learning about best practices and ground-breaking research on African-American males. Vice Provost Valerie B. Lee calls the BRC one of the Office of Diversity and Inclusion's "most promising initiatives; it's an engine for excellence."

On Friday, October 29, 2010, the Office of Minority Affairs underwent one of its most significant changes to date. As Dr. Lee notes, "Understanding that the business of the office had become far more expansive than the term 'minority' implied, and that the name no longer fits with what we are, what we do, or what we can become, the Board of Trustees voted to approve changing the name of our office to the Office of Diversity and Inclusion. This change embraces our legacy and mission and places us in the position to help set the national agenda for discussions about diversity and inclusion. Our new name does not mean we will stray from our core mission; rather it means we will continue to fulfill that mission in the context of a changing world, meeting the challenges and shaping the future of a 21st century society."

The Office of Diversity and Inclusion is very proud of its four-decade commitment and looks forward to building on its powerful legacy.

Office of Diversity and Inclusion ***Executive Council***

"Since its inception, our office has understood true education and diversity to be inseparable, interdependent and inextricable."

-Valerie B. Lee
Vice Provost and Chief Diverity Officer

THE HISTORY OF THE FRANK W. HALE, JR. BLACK CULTURAL CENTER AT THE OHIO STATE UNIVERSITY

By Frank W. Hale, Jr., Ph.D. 

I consider it a great honor and a very great distinction to have had the privilege and opportunity of having the Frank W. Hale, Jr. Black Cultural Center named in my honor. I must express my appreciation to President Edward H. Jennings and the Board of Trustees during my tenure for helping to make that possible. It was in 1982 that Dr. Jennings made a commitment to establish a Black Cultural Center on the campus. The university secured the services of three local African-American architects to renovate Bradford Commons, which had been used as a dining facility, as the project area. Nearly $400,000 was designated to begin the initiative, and the architects generously contributed the funds accorded them to establish scholarships for African-American students in the School of Architecture. Those architects who exhibited such racial pride were Curtis Moody, John Coke, John Spencer and Howard Nolan.

An irresistible sense of reflection and awe wells up within me when I think of the student pioneers, some of whom sacrificed their education and careers, to make it possible for other Black students and Black faculty and staff to be recruited for this campus as a prelude to the establishment of the Center. They stood for and with unwavering patience and perseverance, met the demands of the emergency of underrepresentation and lack of diversity. We must place them high on the historical pinnacle of sacrifice, honor and gratitude. They deserve our appreciation, our applause, and much, much, more!

A decade before in 1972, students and faculty under the leadership of Dr. William E. Nelson, Jr., then chairman of the department of Black Studies, had been vocal in their support and in their insistence that a Black Cultural Center become a reality on The Ohio State University Campus. Numerous students paid the price of being dismissed because of their demonstrative efforts in support of the Center. It was debated as to whether the Center should be under the administration of Black Studies, Student Affairs or Minority Affairs. At the time, central administration, favoring Student Affairs, neglected to support the establishment of the Center by taking advantage of the division that existed among various African and African-American constituencies on campus.

A plebiscite among African-American students and faculty overwhelmingly supported the idea of the Center being under the administration of Minority Affairs. Lacking in administration support, the project lay stalled and frozen until 1982.

I, along with Dr. William E. Nelson, Jr. and Dr. Mac Stewart reopened the issue of the need for a Black Cultural Center on campus with President Jennings and Dr. Diether Haenicke, then provost in 1982. "We solicited their support, asking them to join with us in our efforts: (1) to create a place where students could come to have a comfortable home away home; (2) to help students learn how to negotiate the operation of the institution by meeting with older students who had already experienced the ins and outs of the university; (3) to provide a place where students could begin to understand, appreciate and celebrate the contributions of Africans and African Americans; and (4) to have a site for opportunities for transracial contacts that would promote healthy race and ethnic relations."

For some of us, it was apparent that in order for Black students to succeed in an immense sea of whiteness on a major university campus and make gains that were necessary for them to persist to the point of graduation, it was essential to create some kind of survival apparatus that would enable them to enhance their hopes and dreams with dignity. The Center's intent was to be a major family room, a home away from home, for Black students who could seek shelter from social isolation, cultural discrimination and the loneliness which minimal numbers create. It would represent an opportunity for "brothers "and "sisters" to come together to affirm, to assert, to enunciate, to emphasize, to propose, to contend and to give voice to their concerns.

Additionally, students would be able to meet and enjoy educational and social exchanges, determine causes for common advocacy, join hands as mentors, mentees, and protégés to be instructed and to learn how to negotiate the university-wide system and to create bonds with allies – Whites, Hispanics, Asians and Native Americans.

The Center is a magnificent monument that declares that neither the university nor we as Black people claim exempt status from those who seek legitimacy within the fabric of the American ideal, and whose American dream remains unmet. It is a serious attempt to deal with a serious need, the need to increase and expand the pool of Black scholars across the landscape of disciplines from art to zoology. It stands as co-curricular to enlarge the canons and boundaries of study, scholarship and to serve as a laboratory of leadership for Black students at The Ohio State University.

The notion of a Black Cultural Center allowed it to serve as a focal point and as a forum for Black constituents to rediscover their origins, reshape their identity, and deal in precise ways with our Africaness, our particular culture and history without being apologetic. From the onset, the Center focused on the efficacy and vitality of the Black experience, Black history and its validity. Those who neither know nor celebrate their history are defenseless, and run the risk of allowing others to interpret the advancement of their ancestry. During my high school days, it was not uncommon to observe the extent to which an entire landscape of Black literature was denied a place in corporate literature. If I had not focused and well-read parents at home, the genius of such brilliant writers as Frances Harper, Phillis Wheatley, James Weldon Johnson, Claude McKay, Arna Bontemps, Countee Cullen, Paul Lawrence Dunbar and W.E.B. DuBois would have confined me to unwarranted ignorance.

Fortunately, President Jennings supported our vision. At the beginning, only about one-half of Bradford Commons (approximately 10, 000 square feet) was allocated for the Center because the other half was being used as a major kitchen to prepare meals for senior citizens throughout Columbus, Ohio, and Franklin County. However, Dr. Jennings promised that when the other half became available, it would be allocated for the Center as well. At the time it was estimated that it would take nearly $1.5 million dollars to make the Center what it should be in terms of space and utilization. The official opening of the first half of the Center took place October 11, 1989, under the leadership of Ms. Teresa Drummond (who later become Dr. Teresa Drummond). It was a dream that helped to create a campus community situation where many African-American students felt comfortable. The Black Cultural Center was located in the heart of the campus, unlike numerous other centers on other college and university campuses where they had often been placed on the perimeter of the campus in a small facility with inadequate space.

The location of the Center had a positive effect within the Black community both on and off the campus. It was less than a block away from the Ohio Student Union, the Law School, The Honors House, and University College. It was only a few yards away from a battery of residence halls, making it available to students who were housed there, and who wished to enjoy the activities of the Center.

The activities of the Hale Center have encompassed the local Columbus community as well as the campus community. The Center has been able to actively engage celebrated leaders to come and share their wisdom with students on campus. They have included Harry Belafonte, Ron Brown, Samuel D. Procter, Bernice King, Randall Robinson, Michael Dyson, Susan Taylor and Cornel West, among many others. Special panels and forums have been held on issues that are pertinent to youth. The Center has also been the focal point for musical entertainment. Local musicians, the campus gospel choir and noted vocal and instrumental groups have also provided entertainment from time to time.

It provides a cultural geography that transcends its physical facility and helps Black students to bear the burdens of their daily struggles.

Black student groups and organizations were also very instrumental in the growth and development of the Center. After years of slow movement on the expansion of Hale Hall, student groups such as Just-Us, Afrikans Committed to Improve our Nation (A.C.T.I.O.N.) and the African Student Union (ASU) helped to make the total physical structure of Hale Hall a reality. On May 19, 1992, over 500 Afrikan American students under the leadership of A.C.T.I.O.N. met with President E. Gordon Gee in the Frank W. Hale, Jr. Black Cultural Center to reconfirm the commitment and completion of Hale Hall. President Gee made Hale Hall a priority in the next capital campaign.

The Afrikan Student Union (ASU) established in 1996 challenged the University and each administration after President Gee with student protests and the longest sit-in in University history with the Hale Center as a point of contention. The completion of Hale Hall was a high priority of ASU's agenda. In the spring of 2000, the second half of the Center became available for use. The official opening of Phase II took place on April of that year. Reverend Leon Sullivan was the keynote speaker for the occasion. During his administration beginning in 1999, Dr. William Kirwan supported the Center philosophically and financially, continuing the work President Gee began. President Kirwan's reputation for fairness and equal opportunity had been firmly established prior to his coming as he had served as president of the University of Maryland, College Park. Early in his administration at Ohio State, he stated that his mission was "Excellence Through Diversity." He also focused on a strong academic agenda in setting significant goals for the University. It was his vision that led to the establishment of the Kirwan Institute on Race.

Whereas the first half of the Center had been devoted primarily to social and cultural programs and events, the second half of the Center focused on academic programs and activities. Financial contributions from the Longaberger Company, Nationwide Insurance and All-American basketball star Jim Jackson totaling over $350,000 has helped to renovate and maintain the Hale Center as one of the finest physical structures in the country. The Center is a holistic marriage that attempts to meet the cultural, social and academic needs of students. The newest part of the Center includes two classrooms as a part of the regular scheduling venues of the campus, a library study area, a seminar conference room, a tutorial room, a large computer laboratory housing 27 computers, a vending eating area, and three administrative offices. The corridor walls are alive with paintings and artistic works of legendary figures like Samella Lewis, Elizabeth Catlett, Sam Gilliam, and a number of contemporary artists like Pheoris West, Larry Collins and Charles Hollingworth, Jr.

Larry Williamson, Jr., the director of the Hale Center since 1992 combines a compassionate regard for students with an engaging energy that keeps the Center buzzing with one indispensable contribution after another. It is open to all students, faculty and citizens without regard to race or ethnicity. A number of local organizations have actively supported and used the Center including The Columbus Links Incorporated, The Columbus Post, The NAACP, and The King Arts Complex, as well as fraternities and sororities.

The Center's annual Thanksgiving Dinner for students was initiated in 1993 to serve 25 students who remained on campus. The Kroger Company was the sponsor of this annual event in its initial stage and U. S. Food Service has been instrumental in maintaining the legacy established by Kroger. The succulence of baked turkey, sweet potatoes, stuffing, corn, greens, relishes, rolls, an assortment of pies, offer a warm and welcoming opportunity for all who attend, representing the various areas of the world from which many students come. The Thanksgiving celebration has grown significantly over the years and now serves nearly 2,000 students each year in the ballrooms of the Ohio Union.

Dr. Hale serves Thanksgiving dinner to students at the Ohio Union

What is also especially significant about the Hale Center is that it provides employment opportunities for over 100 college work-study students and up to six graduate students. It has been the undaunted service of administrative secretary, Leona Smith; development officer, Wanda White; receptionist, LaShalle Johnson; and program manager, Ron Parker along with the unflagging dedication of Larry Williamson, Jr., and the student support that has kept the Center vital on a day-to-day basis. Vice Provosts, Hale, Leroy Pernell, Mac Stewart and Valerie Lee have provided invaluable guidance, experience, and inspiration in the growth and advancement of the Center during their tenure.

The challenge for every Black student who comes to The Ohio State University campus is to take advantage of what the Black Cultural Center can offer -

- **By stepping into life with vigor and expectation.**
- **By stepping up in life with your goals and aspirations.**
- **By stepping into life and confronting the obstacles that would impede your progress.**
- **By stepping into life not outside of life, and not be afraid to challenge the ridiculous.**

- Dr. Frank W. Hale, Jr.

Tell the cynics that without Black History, there is no Black Culture. Without Black Culture, there is no Black Dignity. Without Black Dignity, there is no Black Pride. Without Black Pride, there is no Black Freedom. And without Black Freedom, you are at the mercy of them to tell you who you are, what your history is, what you're worth, and what you will become. The day will come when you will speak loud and clear, but it will not be the history that will be taught in London, Paris, Rome, Moscow, Washington or the United Nations. It will be the history that will be taught by those who have won their freedom, step by step, brick by brick, novel by novel, concerto by concerto, symphony by symphony, and scientific wonder by scientific wonder. It will be history by those who possess the corpuscles of courage and the antibodies of adventure that will help to transform the landscape of the world.

Dr. Frank W. Hale, Jr. pictured with Larry Williamson, Director of the Frank W. Hale, Jr. Hale Black Cultural Center

Hale Hall
Frank W. Hale, Jr.
Black Cultural Cen
153 West 12th Ave

OHIO

UNION

Sharing collaborative efforts to bring about pride, performance and a phenomenal project at **The Ohio State University ... The Ohio Union**

MOODY•NOLAN

CURTIS J. MOODY, FAIA, NCARB, LEED AP
PRESIDENT AND CEO

Moody•Nolan has been intimately involved with The Ohio State University's plans for a new Student Union from the earliest stages of the project. The firm worked closely with the university to prepare a preliminary analysis and feasibility study. At the same time the firm worked with the Union's administrators to develop a series of conceptual plans and visualizations that became a mainstay of the early fundraising efforts.

The new Ohio Union is a truly innovative and groundbreaking example of the building type. To begin with, it is large - one of the largest student unions in the nation. Its wide ranging accommodations include a food court in addition to a number of stand-alone food/ beverage venues; a concert hall and large/small performance spaces; a truly massive ballroom capable of innumerable incarnations; numerous conference and meeting rooms; and a large and extremely well appointed suite of student organization offices.

All of these spaces key off, and are supported by, a barrel vaulted, dramatically tall and airy, Great Hall. This dynamic space is both the organizational spine and conceptual heart of the entire facility. School pride and pride of place are in evidence from the moment one grasps the O H-I O front door pulls. Scarlet and Gray threads are woven throughout the facility and the iconic Block "O" and Buckeye Leaf can be found in numerous and varied expressions.

The New Ohio Union achieved LEED Silver certification from the US Green Building Council, a designation that would place it in the upper echelon of collegiate unions in terms of sustainable design.

LEWIS R. SMOOT, JR.
SENIOR VICE PRESIDENT

Smoot Construction has had an opportunity to work on numerous projects at The Ohio State University and we believe the Ohio Union showcases the abilities and expertise of a team that constantly strives to "Perform with Excellence to Maximize Client Success".

Smoot Construction and Moody•Nolan have a long-standing relationship and successful track record. Through nearly 30 years of collaboration, we have developed a highly-effective and productive team synergy that is based upon a mutual respect and appreciation of each other's process and approach.

Our collaborative efforts on this project was no exception and we believe The Ohio State University, its president, faculty and students will all agree that this student facility is one of the top of its kind in the country.

We are pleased to be a 100% family-owned, African-American business that had the privilege to participate as the Construction Manager with Moody•Nolan and The Ohio State University to complete this award-winning project

Columbus • Indianapolis • Washington DC

Continuing the legacy ...
A Three-Generation Corporation

Experience • Integrity • Results

Sherman R. Smoot
Founder (Deceased)

Lewis R. Smoot, Sr.
Chairman & CEO

Mark S. Cain
President

Lewis R. Smoot, Jr.
Sr. Vice President

Richard R. Smoot
Field Operations

Dana Smoot
Asst. Vice President
General Counsel

The Smoot Corporation is the parent company of its operations in Columbus, Ohio and Indianapolis, Indiana, and is a privately-held corporation. In addition to the Smoot Corporation, the Smoot family owns the Smoot Construction Company of Washington, D.C. These entities trace their roots back to 1946 and the commercial masonry contracting business established by our founder, Sherman R. Smoot in Charleston, West Virginia. In 1956, Mr. Smoot moved the company to Columbus.

Today, the three corporate entities offer a comprehensive range of general contracting, design/build and construction management services to public and private clients throughout the Midwest, the Ohio River Valley and the Mid-Atlantic Region.

Milestone Dates

- 1946 Sherman R. Smoot Company (Masonry Contractor) - Established in Charleston WV
- 1956 Operations relocated to Columbus OH
- 1967 Operations established in Washington DC
- 1972 Operations expanded to include general contracting
- 1991 Operations established in Indianapolis IN
- 2011 The Smoot Corporation is registered to perform services for clients in the District of Columbia, Illinois, Indiana, Kentucky, Louisiana, Maryland, Ohio, Pennsylvania, Tennessee and Virginia with a full time staff of approximately 135 professionals.

These companies have grown and flourished because of the high standards of the entire Smoot team which extend through all phases of construction including knowledgeable needs assessment, thorough on-site supervision, responsible and effective office management, and successful project completion.

We are proud that this has been our experience and reputation since 1946!

"The lessons of the past are the blueprints of the future."
Sherman R. Smoot, Founder

Columbus • Indianapolis • Washington DC

Smoot Construction was privileged to have an opportunity to work with The Ohio State University as masonry contractors, general contractors, and now proudly as construction managers having just completed the new Ohio Union.

We have highlighted project photos and listed some of the projects we participated in over the last 50 years at The Ohio State University.

Arps Hall Parking Garage

Clinical Medical Building

Graduate and Student Housing

Jessie Owens Stadium

Law Building

Mershon Auditorium

Neuropsychiatric Building

Parks Hall

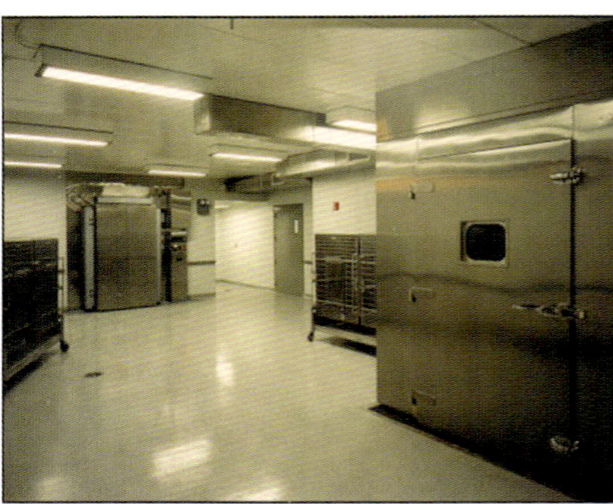
Primate Research Facility

Columbus • Indianapolis • Washington DC

Our Guiding Principles are CHIPP

Character, Humility, Integrity, Pride and Performance

These principles help us identify, hire and retain the best people. They motivate in us a commitment to accountability which fosters repeat business. And they give us strength in reaching out and actively supporting the communities in which we work and live.

Psychology Building

Ross Heart Hospital

The James Cancer Center

The Ohio Union

University Hospital Helipad

Lincoln Towers

William Oxley Thompson Library

Wiseman Hall

Other projects completed at
The Ohio State University

12th Avenue Parking Garage
Arthritis Center
Lazenby Hall
Postle Hall
Rightmire Hall
Stadium Dorm

Ohio State University alumni The Honorable Yvette McGee Brown is sworn in as Ohio's first African-American female Supreme Court Justice by Governor Ted Strickland. January 8, 2011

OFFICE OF UNIVERSITY OUTREACH & ENGAGEMENT

Our stories and history are a gateway to the programs, resources, and partnerships through which The Ohio State University provides outreach and engagement with communities across the street and around the globe.

Outreach & Engagement at The Ohio State University signifies a marriage of scholarship and service, where the talents and knowledge developed at the university are utilized to address the major issues of our society. The focus is to build partnerships and collaborations with mutual and significant impact for the university and our local, state, national and global communities. The office supports innovative and creative outreach and engagement initiatives that connect academic excellence with societal needs. It enhances and/ or creates partnerships between members of the university community and community partners, and it enhances the development of a unit's outreach and engagement mission.

Roads Scholars Tour 2009 Group Shot

The Ohio State University was one of the American institutions of higher learning established under the first landmark Morrill Act of 1862. The Morrill Act was intended to provide a broad segment of the population with a practical education that had direct relevance to their daily lives. Through the land-grant university heritage, millions of students are able to study every academic discipline and explore fields of inquiry far beyond the scope envisioned in the original land-grant mission. America's land-grant universities continue to fulfill their democratic mandate for openness, accessibility and service to people, and like Ohio State, many of these institutions join the ranks of the nation's most distinguished public engaged and research universities.

Joyce Beatty, Senior Vice President
Office of University Outreach & Engagement

The emphasis on being an engaged university began in 1994, when President E. Gordon Gee led the inception of a vision and values for Ohio State's outreach mission. A key piece of their work was defining "outreach" through a three-fold mission: *Outreach is that aspect of teaching that enables learning beyond the campus walls. Outreach is that aspect of research that makes what we discover useful beyond the academic community. Outreach is that aspect of service that directly benefits the public.*

The formalized title of "outreach and engagement" came two years later, as a result of President Gee's involvement as chair of the Kellogg Commission on the Future of State and Land-Grant Universities.

The definition now begins: *"Outreach & Engagement is defined as a meaningful and mutually beneficial collaboration with partners in education, business, and public and social service."*

In 2009, President Gee made Outreach & Engagement a senior management-level office at the university and appointed former Ohio House of Representatives Minority Leader Joyce Beatty as its senior vice president, making her the first African-American female to serve at that level. In the rapidly-changing 21st-century world, President Gee saw the import of bringing the university's storied knowledge generation and research prominence to bear on the economic, educational, and social issues facing communities.

Medical Center Expansion Rendering

The Office of Outreach & Engagement places its fingerprints on the movement *From Excellence to Eminence* with projects covering many diverse areas, including international partnership, economic advancement, health care, continuing education, government, minority business development, and lifelong learning. Its sphere of influence transcends colleges and units, creating broad partnerships that leverage the expertise and passions of Ohio State's faculty, staff, and students.

Equal opportunity is a basic philosophy at The Ohio State University, and Outreach & Engagement actively supports the commitment to encourage business opportunities and diversity among its vendors. The office encourages and participates in the continued growth and development of purchasing goods and services from State of Ohio-certified Minority Business Enterprises (MBE) and certified Encouraging Diversity, Growth and Equity (EDGE) businesses. These efforts have opened doors for women and minorities and have heightened awareness and economic benefits.

Outreach & Engagement is involved in the university's mission through several major initiatives to improve lives for generations. The office works with projects that engaged residents and faculty in the University District's Weinland Park neighborhood, which has struggled under the weight of poverty, unemployment, poor housing, and lack of access to job opportunities and nutritious foods. Trans-institutional partnerships are helping to transform this community through a multipronged approach. Job training and employment outreach programs are helping residents develop the skills to be competitive in the working world. The Volunteer Income Tax Assistance program – in which law and business students offer free tax preparation services to low- and moderate-income working individuals – has recovered more than $2.3 million in earned income and tax credit for more than 1,500 families. Outreach & Engagement proudly selected this important work to compete for regional and national honors through the 2011 C. Peter Magrath University / Community Engagement Awards.

Likewise, Outreach & Engagement is involved in an historic $1 billion Medical Center expansion project that will enhance medical services, research, and teaching across central Ohio, the state, and the nation. This includes a $25 million investment in the predominantly African-American community around University Hospital East on Columbus' Near East Side that will focus on expanded health care services and improved housing. The office is also at the forefront of coordinating the President's African-American Ministers Group, which focuses on improving the quality of health care, education, and wellness exposure for African-American families.

Engaging our students is a critical piece of Outreach & Engagement's success. The office is an engaged partner in the oversight of the university's nationally-renowned Service-Learning Initiative, which engages thousands of Ohio State students in more than 70 courses that combine classroom theory and community practice.

Society of Sisters funded by JPMorgan Chase

These students give thousands of hours outside class to "pay it forward" and better their communities. Service-learning now satisfies general education requirements for undergraduate students, encouraging them even further to integrate experiential learning into their curricula.

The Office has also created programming to augment the development of Ohio State students into the leaders, thinkers, and innovators of tomorrow. A partnership with a 50-member African-American female student organization called Society of Sisters developed into a Leadership Academy funded in the first year by JPMorgan Chase. The academy teaches the participants about several aspects of leadership, from public speaking and preparation for a world of culture change to networking and career development. These students were honored through another Outreach & Engagement partnership: the unveiling of the 2010 edition of *Who's Who In Black Columbus.* This partnership started with the publisher of this book and continues with the present publishers to sponsor a community reception that attracts some 800 prominent African-Americans and others to the university. The publication itself contains a featured Ohio State section highlighting African-American academic and administrative university leaders.

Ohio State's outreach and engagement footprint extends to every corner of Ohio, a fact that is shared with new faculty and administrators every year during the Roads Scholars Tour. This event has become part of the orientation tradition for new faculty and administrators, who embark on a two-day traveling seminar to witness how Ohio State's teaching and research are benefitting communities. Many of the projects featured on the tours are recipients of Engagement Impact Grants, seed grants that have helped leverage more than $3 million in additional private funding support for impactful projects.

Rosa Parks Day Statewide Tribute

Outreach & Engagement initiated and authored a school transformation/turnaround plan that is federally-funded to enhance the learning atmosphere and support sustained student achievement for students in primary and secondary schools. This $3 million partnership with the Ohio Department of Education creates the Executive Principals Leadership Academy, an intensive executive management program for school principals provided through the Fisher College of Business, in partnership with the Office of Academic Affairs and the College of Education and Human Ecology. Many of the schools served by this program are located in minority communities that represent great opportunity for inspirational leadership and transformative education.

In recognition of the legends and legacies of the many African-American alumni from Ohio State, whose accomplishments and civil rights efforts led to the quality of life and standards we have today, we highlight Outreach & Engagement's leadership and coordination of the annual Rosa Parks Day Statewide Tribute, "The Power of One." This education and awareness program for thousands of elementary school children teaches that Mrs. Parks' past is prelude to pursuing a future of equality and opportunity for all. This tribute honors Ohio's standing as the first state in the nation to designate December 1 as Rosa Parks Day. (H.B. 421, *authored by Joyce Beatty, Ohio House of Representatives, 2005).*

Part of Outreach & Engagement's responsibility is to explore potential collaborations outside Ohio and outside the United States. In 2010, the Office led a first-of-its-kind Internationalizing Outreach journey to Ghana in West Africa, where a leadership delegation of administrators, faculty and students explored partnerships in nutrition, health care, agriculture, and distance learning. The delegation met with leaders in three government ministries (Health, Agriculture, and Education) and engaged with dignitaries at three prominent universities. This engagement established a relationship with eight Ghanaian Ohio State alumni who are teaching and / or leading at these universities! This common bond is producing new, mutually-beneficial opportunities for partnership across the Atlantic Ocean with the University of Cape Coast and the University of Education – Winneba.

Outreach & Engagement salutes *From Excellence to Eminence... 100 Years of African-American Achievement at The Ohio State University* for its commitment to engaging the university community and immortalizing the impact of its faculty, staff, and students in communities across central Ohio and around the world. The partnerships featured in these pages remind us all of a legacy we cherish and a foundation upon which to build.

Ohio State University brought us together and we are friends for LIFE! Andrea Attaway-Young (right) and Pam Tapscott-Lassiter met as freshman and graduated together, Friday, June 13, 1980. Who said Friday the 13th was unlucky? Andrea and Pam wanted to make sure Ohio State University was recognized, as the country welcomed the 44th President of the United States, Barack Obama during inaugural ceremonies held January 20, 2009 near the grounds of the Washington Monument!

The Black Experience in Student Affairs

The history of Student Affairs at The Ohio State University has remarkably evolved for students, support services and the face of its leadership. When Ohio State opened its doors in 1873, students of color were not included in its inaugural class; yet today, the campus community welcomes students and staff from across the world. From a single unit that was responsible for providing support to all students, Student Life is now comprised of more than 30 departments, 1,000 student organizations, and 5,000 employees (including 4,000 student workers), that work together to ensure that Ohio State students graduate having had extraordinary experiences as Buckeyes.

Until 1944, all services that are now part of Student Affairs reported directly to the President. There was no Vice President for Student Affairs—much of that responsibility was handled by the Dean of Men and the Dean of Women, who each reported to the President. Between 1890 and 1930, most of the other services we know today got started. The Athletic Board was created in 1890 and recreational sports began in 1906. An admissions office was formally organized in 1905, and the student health service began in 1908. Mothers' Clubs and Dads' Clubs were also formed during this era.

Gradually, professional staff were added to undertake responsibilities for out-of-classroom activities and student services. For the first 90 years or so, until the late 1960s, many student services were divided by sex—with a Dean of Men and Dean of Women operating more or less parallel operations overseeing housing, student organizations, discipline, student governance, etc.

The first student union, now Enarson Hall, was opened in 1910 and allotted spaces for student organizations. The union was only for male students. Pomerene Hall was built in 1922 as a union for women students. When the Ohio Union opened in 1951, it was for all students.

Dr. Javaune Adams-Gaston,
Vice President for Student Life

With regard to students of color, the experience would become more holistic after the Great Depression, as for many years, OSU residence halls did not accept black students. In 1942, limited residential living opportunities were made available for African-American students. Even though Ohio State made its commitment to students of color known, a number of local rooming houses still did not rent rooms to blacks until 1957, as pushes began to be made to end discrimination in all housing endorsed by the university, including fraternities and sororities, and in student government and other activities. Various improvements were made during the 1960s, but it was not until 1969 that the university formally adopted an open housing rule forbidding discrimination in all university supported and endorsed housing.

The first steps toward an advocacy office for minority students occurred in 1968, when Vice President Mount named a special assistant for minority affairs as part of his restructuring of the area of Student Affairs, due particularly to the voices of black students and his expressed desire to ensure that every Ohio State student received access to the resources that would enhance their experience, both academically and beyond the classroom.

The student affairs organization would continue to expand its support for minority students, as evidenced by entities such as the Multicultural Center and the various support units within Student Life (as it is currently known).

Today, Ohio State's Office of Student Life continues to connect the points where the university intersects with students' lives, bringing the experience full-circle from the classroom and professional development to home and play. The overarching goal of the Office of Student Life is to enhance the student experience and promote student success.

Every department in Student Life touches students' lives in a unique way, and the programs and services are designed to accommodate a wide range of student needs.

Our current senior leader for the Office of Student Life (as it is now known), holds a place in Ohio State history, as she, Dr. Javaune Adams-Gaston, was named OSU's first female Vice President for Student Life.

First African-American Homecoming Queen (1960)
Marlene Owens also the daughter of Olympian Jesse Owens

Currently, Javaune, or Dr. J, as she is affectionately called, oversees the operations of the Office of Student Life and its constituent departments. She has broad leadership responsibility for numerous university operations affecting students outside the classroom, including residence halls, food service, the Ohio Union and student activities, student leadership development, mental health counseling, career direction, recreational sports, health care and wellness programs, disability services, the Multicultural Center, off-campus student services, the student judicial process, and student advocacy and crisis intervention. She represents Student Life in the university's senior administration and provides leadership on issues affecting students. Dr. J's leadership exemplifies the Office of Student Life's commitment to diversity and its focus on the success of all students, as noted by the wide offering of support services, programming, a dedicated staff and a primary goal of ensuring that students receive a holistic educational experience.

History serves as a fine example of how African-American students and leaders have left their mark within the university community, and the Office of Student Life at The Ohio State University is proud to help serve as the vehicle in the defining of many victories and legacies.

First Black Greek Fraternity: Alpha Phi Alpha Fraternity, Incorporated-Kappa Chapter

First Black Student Organization (1910)
The Omusu Club was founded, which would later become the Kappa Chapter of Alpha Phi Alpha Fraternity, Incorporated.

First Black Greek Fraternity: Alpha Phi Alpha Fraternity, Incorporated-Kappa Chapter
The Kappa Chapter of Alpha Phi Alpha was chartered on January 13, 1911, making it the tenth chapter created by the first of the nine National Panhellenic organizations. Kappa Chapter charter members were James A. Dunn, L.H. Hatchcock, Clarence A. Jones, J.C. Kingslow, W.O. Stokes, Fred Holsey and C.P. Lyman. Also among the Kappa Chapter members is the legendary Olympian Jesse Owens.

Our Choking Times
Newsmagazine
SERVING THE UNDERSERVED
The Ohio State University
October 1979

First Black Student Newspaper
Our Choking Times (1970, no longer in print).

Delta Sigma Theta Sorority, Incorporated-Epsilon Chapter Founders
Bernice N. Copeland, Phila Ann McGillery White, Catherine Thompson Alexander, Fairy Shores Burrell, and Alberta Hanley.

First Black Sorority: Delta Sigma Theta Sorority, Incorporated-Epsilon Chapter
The Epsilon Chapter was welcomed to the Ohio State campus on November 19, 1919, and was founded by five dedicated young women: Bernice N. Copeland, Phila Ann McGillery White, Catherine Thompson Alexander, Fairy Shores Burrell, and Alberta Hanley. Today, Epsilon Chapter hosts numerous activities and programs committed to serving the campus and the community.

First Black Student Body President: Michael R. White (1970)

He also earned a Bachelor of Arts degree in 1973 and a Master of Public Administration degree in 1974. Upon his Ohio State graduation, White returned to Cleveland, where he served the Cleveland City Council as an administrative assistant from 1976 to 1977 and later served as city councilman from the Glenville district from 1978 to 1984. During his tenure in city council, White became a well-known protégé of Councilman George L. Forbes. White then represented the area's 21st District in the Ohio Senate, serving as a Democratic Assistant Minority Whip. In 1990 he bacame the 55th Mayor of Cleveland, Ohio and served as Mayor until 2002.

Office of Black Student Services Founded in 1969
Georgina Bowman, Ph.D., an Ohio State graduate would serve as its first director.

Student Affairs Facilities Named in Honor of Olympian Jesse Owens (1976)
Jesse Owens cemented his name in the history and fabric of Student Affairs facilities when three buildings were dedicated in his honor, including the Jesse Owens Recreation Center-North, the Jesse Owens West Tennis Center and the Jesse Owens Recreation Center-South. Today, all three facilities continue to draw thousands of students and visitors yearly, and continue to represent Jesse's tenacious spirit, love for recreation and sports, and his ultimate commitment to Ohio State.

Ohio Union Selects its First African-American Director (1994)
Rebecca Parker, Ph.D., was named as director for the Ohio Union in 1994, and would help shape student activities and student organizations through 2001.

First Black Vice President for Student Life/Vice Provost for Student Affairs (1984)
In 1984, Student Life would welcome its first African-American senior leader, as Russell Spillman was named Vice Provost for Student Affairs and then Vice President of the same office. As the Vice Provost and Vice President, Spillman provided leadership to the campus and students with regard to the non-academic components of student life. Spillman would serve Ohio State in student services from 1984 to 1993, at which point he returned to the Ohio State faculty.

In 1993, President Gee named David Williams, JD, as Vice President for Student Affairs, a position he would hold from 1993 through 2000 as Student Affairs' second African-American senior leader.

Dr. D'Andra Mull
Chief of Staff and Director of Graduate Programming and Special Projects

Colin Brown
Senior Director of Student Life Development

Dr. Lance Kennedy-Phillips
Director of Student Life Research and Assessment

Lois Harris
Director of Disability Services

Willie Young
Director of Off-Campus Housing

2011 African Americans in Student Life

The 2011 leadership of the Office of Student Life reflects a strong commitment to diversity, as reflected in the make-up of Ohio State's Office of Student Life senior leadership team has evolved over the years, growing from only one African-American representative in 1969 to seven African-American leaders in 2011.

Without question, students have also provided a voice and guidance with regard to how they best feel supported, and continue to be integral to the development of the programs and services. From organizations such as the Undergraduate Student Government and the Sphinx Senior Honorary, to the Black Student Association and the African American Heritage Festival Committee, African-American students have served as leaders on campus and beyond, and continue to serve as fine examples of The Ohio State University.

Ohio State University Class of 2010 African American graduates.

A Colorful Collection of Memories and Facts

By Debora R. Myles '80 

Attention, Roll Call!

AKA, AΦA, ΔΣθ, IΦθ, KAΨ, ΩΨΦ, ΦΒΣ, ΣΓΡ, ZΦΒ. "The Divine Nine" is the unique nickname of distinction given to the Black Greek Letter Organizations (BGLOs) that are collectively known as the National Pan-Hellenic Council. These four sororities and five fraternities are the pioneers for the black fraternal social/service organizations on college campuses across the United States. This rich African-American history begins in 1906 with the "grand daddies," the men of Alpha Phi Alpha Fraternity, Inc. on the campus of Cornell University. The final member of The Divine Nine is Iota Phi Theta formed in 1963 on Morgan State University's campus. The initial BGLOs were incorporated and local chapters were established on both black and predominantly white college campuses. These organizations became the cornerstone for black coeds by providing camaraderie, social and athletic activities, leadership skills and support systems for tackling issues on campus, in the community and ultimately in the workforce.

The invasion of The Divine Nine struck OSU when sorors and bruhs established chapters on the yard between January 13, 1911, and April 16, 1988. It should be noted, Beta Kappa Alpha Fraternity, Inc. (BKA) was founded at OSU in 1976, as an alternative to The Elite 8 — the predecessor to The Divine Nine.

The Good, The Bad, The Awesome Future: 1910s and 1920s

As white America entered the Decade of Tomorrow and the Roaring Twenties, black coeds at OSU were experiencing, The Good, The Bad and The Awesome Future.

January 13, 1911, was a good day when seven men chartered Alpha Phi Alpha Fraternity (AΦA), Kappa Chapter and became the tenth chapter and first black fraternity at OSU.

Quickly, these men gained national prominence by hosting the 5th National Convention, electing charter member Clarence A. Jones as a National General Treasurer; charter member James A. Dunn designed the national shield.

OSU enjoyed another good day when five ladies chartered Epsilon Chapter of Delta Sigma Theta Sorority (ΔΣθ) on November 19, 1919, making it the fifth chapter and the first black sorority at OSU. The trendsetting Deltas were part of an expansion to predominantly white campuses in order to assist students with the injustice of race and gender discrimination. By the 5th National Convention, Epsilon Chapter was the host. Many more good days followed as more Black Greeks arrived at OSU: Kappa Alpha Psi (KAΨ), Zeta Chapter in 1915; Alpha Kappa Alpha (AKA), Theta Chapter in 1921; and Omega Psi Phi (ΩΨΦ), Iota Psi Chapter in 1926.

During these two decades, the NAACP was forming and Black Friday closed out the decade. However, it didn't deter the Greeks at OSU.

James A. Dunn attended The Ohio State Univerisity and became a charter member of the Alpha Phi Alpha, Kappa Chapter in 1911. In 1911, he was the first black architectural engineer to graduate from Ohio State University.

Brother Dunn is credited with designing the Alpha Phi Alpha Fraternity Shield.

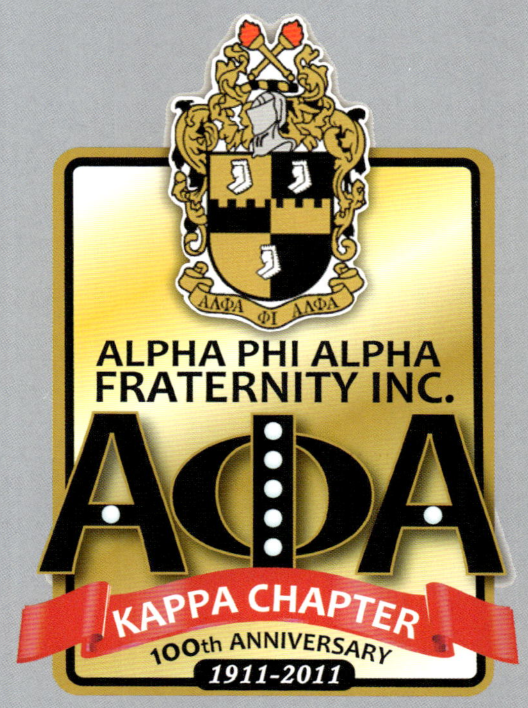

ΔΣΘ
AKA
ΑΦΑ

Instead, they relished in The Good: five Black Greek organizations at OSU, the opportunity to go to college, the establishment of lifelong friendships, off-campus socials, and election of an Alpha, Daniel L. Ferguson, as class orator in 1916, who was also an outstanding athlete. They endured The Bad: overt and covert racism, gender discrimination and an economy that was never on their side. Lastly, they had seen a glimpse of The Awesome Future. It is these five organizations and their members who kicked the door down and laid the cornerstone for future African Americans at OSU to experience and excel in educational, social and recreational, service and political activism.

The Best of Times and the Frustrating of Times: 1930s and 1940s:

As white America entered the Great Depression and the Decade of War, coeds at OSU were still experiencing "Negro Only" in housing, restaurants and hotels. When the fall quarter began in 1933, getting a bite to eat on campus was limited, even for a future Olympian and judge. These future greats were restricted to the Ohio Union, Pomerene Hall, carry-out service or "Negro Only" restaurants in the city.

Mary Carter Glascor and the future Judge H. Alfred Glascor pose on their way to a party.

Black Greeks took their activities off campus because they had no choice; they were not allowed to meet on campus. Mary Carter Glascor, the future wife of Judge Glascor, fondly recalls meeting off campus at the homes of relatives and friends of the coeds to discuss sorority activities. During this time, KOADA — Kappa, Omega, AKA, Delta, Alpha — was founded and served as an on-campus Pan-Hellenic. There were some white students who were empathetic and it was these students who buddied up with KOADA students to go to restaurants to document racism and demonstrate for equality.

By the 1940s, another future judge, Robert Duncan, arrived on campus and pledged Kappa Alpha Psi. It is through the frat he met lifelong friend and OSU and NFL great, William Willis. Duncan recalls the camaraderie and healthy competition among the KOADA Council members. Their "mecca" became the Spring Street YMCA. He recalls Minister Russell Jones, an employee at OSU, who also served as an

In 2011, Robert M. Duncan celebrated his 50th year anninversary as a member of Kappa Alpha Psi Fraternity, Inc.

advisor to KOADA. "Minister Jones was our Frank Hale," states Duncan.

Similar to the 1930s, Pomerene Hall and the Ohio Union were the only places to eat on campus. In the 1940s the second floor of the Ohio Union was the spot to play ping pong, pool and listen to the ladies play the piano. "St. Paul AME Church and Second Baptist were our places for worship and served as a marvelous support system," shares Duncan. "After church we'd eat, conduct our frat meeting and then socialize with the KOADA Council."

The Power of Education and Black Power: 1950s and 1960s

By the 1950s blacks on campus made strides and some became the second generation of college educated. The theme continued during the 1950s and 1960s in that the Black Greeks continued to socialize through dances and athletic events, with the Ohio Union as the focal point. Nannette Sanders Reynolds and her AKA sorors, along with the other members of KOADA, would meet on Monday evening on the second floor of the Ohio Union to conduct sorority and fraternity meetings. During this time the big parties were held at the Pythian Theatre, currently The King Arts Complex.

With the 1960s came a sense of black pride. Cleveland's future mayor and OSU's first Black Student Body President, Michael White, was a Kappa. It is during this time, many of the BGLOs began to do community service projects with local schools and centers in the Columbus area.

In 1968 and 1969, OSU welcomed the Blue and White Family, Zeta Phi Beta, Xi Gamma Chapter and Phi Beta Sigma, Delta Omicron Chapter, respectively.

It had been more than 40 years since a new Black Greek organization had come to the yard. Cora Brown Miller, a 1966 Columbus North High School grad and charter member of Zeta Phi Beta, remembers being initiated by the local grad chapter. She was one on a line of six. They started the pledge process during the fall of 1967 and were initiated in January of 1968. Later that year, three more ladies had chosen Zeta Phi Beta.

OSU Greek Pan-Hellenic Picnic during the Summer of 1960.

The Fruits of the Seeds of Struggle: 1970s and 1980s

The Black Greek fraternities and sororities continued to thrive as a main source of friendship, entertainment and healthy competition. By now, many of the black frats had unofficial houses where frat meetings and social gatherings occurred. However, the Ohio Union continued to be the prime location for meetings, socials and parties. The Ohio Union Ballroom remained the focal point for parties; Bradford Commons and Drake Union become secondary locations; and off-campus apartment party houses become the new hot spot for OSU black coeds.

During this time secret handshakes among the frats, sorority calls and hand gestures for all Black Greeks became the means for greeting your sorors or bruhs and striking a pose.

Black Greeks participated in the OSU block parties — Drake Union during the fall and the Oval during the spring. The block parties were complete with vendors, food, dancing and step shows. Where there were once song fests, the new performance is stepping; all Black Greeks have their own unique steps and chants. Step shows were very popular and took place during competitions, but were also done during Pro Shows, just before the future Greek was initiated and crossed the burning sands. The individual Greek secret rituals implemented for initiation are frequently referred to as "crossing the burning sands." Those that were initiated together, lovingly refer to themselves as "sands."

During the 1970s and 1980s, at some point in time every frat had an interest group. These groups were dedicated ladies whose objective was to support the frat. The ladies interest groups were as follows: Alpha Angels, Beta Blossoms, Kappa Kittens and later Kappa Diamonds, Omega Pearls, and Sigma Sweethearts.

Nanette Sanders Reynolds as the 1960 Alpha Phi Alpha Queen in 1960.

In 1971 Sigma Gamma Rho, Delta Phi, became the fourth and final Black sorority at OSU. Joanne Hart, later known as Mother Love, pledged Sigma Gamma Rho. Mother Love recalls, "I became the women that I am today due to my experiences as a Black Greek on campus."

In 1988, the men of Iota Phi Theta became a chapter at OSU with the pledge class, 1st Born. This first line was pledged by the Iotas from Central State.

If You Can Dream It, You Can Do It: 1990s and 2000s

By 1990, The Divine Nine was representing on campus in ways its predecessors could have never imagined. In 1991 Michael Owens, a Phi Beta Sigma man, became the 1991 Homecoming King, and he was introduced to more than 100,000 people during half-time of the OSU vs. Michigan State football game.

During this time, BGLOs were fully vested in OSU's Greek Week activities. By combining their skills and talents, they were able to compete in sports and perform. This unity carried into the Spring Step Show for the BGLOs, which had moved from the Ohio Union to Hitchcock Hall. All nine organizations competed and a special Divine Nine routine was created that included representatives from all organizations. By the 15th Annual Pan-Hellenic Black Greek Step Show, the popularity was so great it was moved to a bigger venue, The Value City Arena at The Jerome Schottenstein Center.

Black Greeks arrived at OSU in 1911, so it is expected that there would be legacies — children of Black Greek organizations that pledge the same sorority or fraternity that their parent pledged. Alisha Martin is a Delta Sigma Theta legacy. She was number 17 on the D.S.T.r.u.c.t.i.v.e 17 pledge line that was initiated fall of 2008. She quickly embraced her sorority's initiatives and enjoyed the camaraderie of her sorors and sands. Just as those Black Greeks before her joined a frat or sorority that matched their interests, Black Greeks today continue to experience a life-long brotherhood and sisterhood that can be felt in virtually any setting. Black Greek life has been and will continue to be an inspiration and hope for our college campuses and the world for many years to follow.

The Past, Present, Future: 2010 and Beyond

In 2010 BGLAOSU (Black Greek Letter Alumni at The OSU or www.bglaosu.com) was created to bring the alumni together who pledged in the 70s and 80s. This goal was realized with the first BGLAOSU Homecoming Reunion Weekend, October 22 – 24, 2010.

It seems appropriate to end the story with those who originated the story — the men of Alpha Phi Alpha Fraternity, Inc., Kappa Chapter. During the weekend of January 14 – 17, 2011, the Alphas became the first Black Greeks at OSU to celebrate a 100th year anniversary. Nearly 130 Alphas were registered for the Founder's Day celebration at the Ohio Union where they learned Kappa Chapter would establish a foundation. The AKAs, BKAs, Deltas, Iotas, Kappas, Ques, Sigmas, SGRhos, and Zetas gave "props" to their Greek bruhs. As they walked away from the celebration, one could hear the Alphas' stepping and chanting "Kappa Chapter, Kappa Chapter OSU. If you ain't an Alpha, you must be number two, or three, or four, or even something more!"

Alpha Phi Alpha Fraternity Inc., Kappa Chapter celebrated 100 years at The Ohio State University in January of 2011.

Special Tribute to the Great

James Cleveland Owens

By Jessica A. Johnson, Ph.D.

From a humble beginning breaking up furrows in Oakville, Alabama, to an Ohio State Buckeye breaking world records in collegiate track and field in the mid-1930s, James Cleveland Owens came along at a time when the nation needed a hero. Owens would often say his story could only happen in America years after winning his four gold medals at the 1936 Berlin Olympics. Despite the obstacles of poverty, racism and discrimination he faced as a poor black boy born to sharecroppers in the South, America was a country that still provided him the opportunity to make something of himself.

Many dreams never came to fruition in the cotton and corn fields of Oakville, where backbreaking labor and overwhelming debt crushed the aspirations of countless black farmers who wearily tilled the land. However, Owens, along with his ten siblings, would not be relegated to this fate when his parents, Henry and Emma, decided to move the family to Cleveland, Ohio, around the early 1920s. Floods and the boll weevil had destroyed many crops in southern Alabama during this time. The Owenses, like hundreds of black sharecropping families in neighboring states, took part in the Great Migration and left the region in pursuit of a better life.

Cleveland was one of the popular Midwest cities to settle in for black families leaving the South behind, and it was here that the young Owens was first exposed to an integrated environment. With Jim Crow laws firmly entrenched in Oakville, Owens' interaction with whites had been minimal. In Cleveland, he enrolled in an integrated public school and was able to attend classes regularly since he was no longer working in the fields. Owens got the name Jesse – the name he would be known by for the rest of his life – from his Bolton Elementary School teacher who misunderstood his heavy southern accent.

Owens' athletic talents were discovered at Fairmount Junior High School by Charles Riley, a white physical education teacher who introduced Owens to track and field. Riley left a profound impact on Owens that would not only result in Olympic glory, but also shape the way Owens viewed race relations in America. In his 1960 biography *Blackthink*, Owens recalled that Riley was "the first white man I really knew and without ever trying, he proved to me beyond all proof that a white man can understand – and love – a Negro" (qtd. in Baker 23). In addition to a moderate outlook on race, Owens adopted the accomodationist philosophy of Booker T. Washington.

Owens had developed a hard work ethic early in life due to his childhood years as a sharecropper. This eventually resulted in a strong Washingtonian view of merit (Baker 25), as Owens believed he could achieve anything he set his mind to while maturing under the tutelage of Riley and taking advantage of the education he was receiving at Fairmount. During his junior high years, Owens undoubtedly was being groomed to be a role model beyond the arena of sports.

As Owens continued to develop his athletic gifts, he also remained practical in terms of his outlook for the future. Like many young black men in the 30s, Owens thought learning a skilled trade would be valuable, so he enrolled in East Technical High School. Owens was fortunate to remain in school as all of his older siblings had dropped out, and times were especially hard during the Great Depression. Although his academic focus was now on vocational education, Owens was still heavily involved in sports and he soon became a dominant presence in high school track and field meets. By his junior year at East Tech, he set a world record in the long jump, and as a senior in 1933 he led his team to a national track title.

Cleveland held a parade in his honor to celebrate East Tech's national championship, and as Owens became a household name in the city, colleges and universities began aggressively recruiting him. He had his choices of schools across the country, but decided to attend Ohio State University and stay close to home.

Enrolling in college was another extraordinary accomplishment for Owens because he was the first in his family to graduate from high school. While his academic preparation for university level work was not as rigorous, Owens still entered OSU full of optimism in the fall of 1933. Black students were not allowed to stay on campus, nor were they served in restaurants on High Street, but Owens did not let segregation deter him from his goals. He developed a good relationship with OSU's track coach Larry Synder, who taught Owens how to hone basic sprinting techniques such as fluid arm motion and a firmer starting stance.

Under Synder's instruction, it did not take Owens long to set his mark in the Big Ten. He won all of his events in a conference meet for freshmen, but his most impressive performance by far was in the 1935 Big Ten Championship meet in Ann Arbor. During that competition Owens set world records in five events, one being the long jump, in which he scored beyond 26 feet. The following year Owens set his sights on making the 1936 U.S. Olympic track and field team. By now he was considered among the nation's top sprinters who dominated the sport. His name was continuously mentioned with other elite black track stars such as Ralph Metcalfe, Eulace Peacock and Eddie Tolan. As major college conferences like the Big Ten were gradually allowing African-American athletes to compete on an integrated playing field, race relations in sports were beginning to change, although the professional ranks of baseball and football remained closed to blacks.

The Summer Games of 1936 would provide a global, athletic platform that would enable Owens to transcend race. The stage had already been set with the boxing match earlier that year between German Max Schmeling and Joe Louis.

Louis was defeated in a stunning upset by Schmeling; yet, Louis symbolically bore American democracy on his shoulders when he faced his German opponent, which transitioned him from representing not just blacks but all Americans.

With the Olympics being held in Berlin, the Nazi regime of Adolph Hitler drew criticism in America for its racist theories of Aryan supremacy and treatment of Jews under the Nuremberg Laws.

Owens crushed Hitler's ideology in competition by winning gold in the 100- and 200-meter dashes, the 400-meter relay and the broad jump, where he set a world record that lasted for 25 years. Owens was now an American champion and the myth of Hitler supposedly snubbing him satisfied, as historian William J. Baker points out, "a fundamental need to believe in moral order; the evil Hitler insulting the innocent Owens, but with innocence and virtue winning in the end."

Owens' innocence and virtue, along with his athletic prowess, continued to be on display throughout Europe as he and his teammates competed in additional meets scheduled by the Amateur Athletic Union. However, Owens soon grew tired of his required extra running. He desired to capitalize on his newfound fame due to the numerous offers he was receiving for appearance fees and endorsements. He also had a young family to support, as he had married his high school sweetheart, Minnie Ruth Solomon, the previous year. The couple had a three-year-old daughter named Gloria and Owens was anxious about his financially stability. He left the European tour to return to the United States, and the AAU immediately suspended his amateur status. Upon returning home, Owens unfortunately found out that most of his offers for big time money were not legitimate and he struggled to earn a living. He held menial jobs and even ran against horses in carnival races. His saving grace would be his public speaking skills. As his family would expand to include two more daughters, Marlene and Beverly, Owens had steady work by the time he was in his early 30s.

Owens remained a nationally beloved figure as the years passed from his Berlin triumphs, but when a new generation of black athletes emerged in the 1960s, he found himself at odds with the militancy they championed. Many black athletes of this era were angry and revolutionary, and they viewed sports as a way to showcase their frustrations with racial and economic inequality in America. Owens, on the other hand, still firmly held to his belief in the nation's ideal of meritocracy, maintaining that failure resulted from lack of true grit and effort. In 1968, he was called to mediate for U.S. officials in the Mexico City Olympics after sprinters John Carlos and Tommie Smith gave their black power salute on the medal stand.

Owens' attempts to reason with them were not successful as Carlos and Smith viewed him as an Uncle Tom, a conservative elder out of touch with the "New Negro" of the 60s. Owens handled their criticism with dignity and in many ways it fueled his patriotism even more in his travels on the lecture circuit. He never wavered from his emphasis on the value of hard work, faith in God, and personal responsibility in his speeches to young people and business and civic groups.

As Owens entered the latter stages of his life, he had established a solid legacy as a public servant. He served on many national boards, which included the Boy Scouts of America, and in 1972 Ohio State awarded Owens an honorary doctorate degree in athletic arts. For most of the 70s he served as the senior statesman of the Olympics (Baker 217). Even in his sixties, people still were in awe of his life story and never seemed to become uninterested in hearing about how he overcame tremendous odds. When Owens passed away in 1980 at age 68, then-OSU president Harold Enarson praised him as a man who "exemplified the foundation on which The Ohio State University has been built – opportunity and excellence" (qtd. in Baker 227). Owens no doubt exemplified these qualities not only as one of Ohio State's greatest sons, but also as one of America's greatest citizens.

References

Baker, William J. Jesse Owens: *An American Life.* New York: The Free Press, 1986.
Print.

McMurray, Charles. Personal Interview. Special Assistant to the President and CEO of Ohio State's Alumni Association. Telephone Interview 27 Jan. 2011.

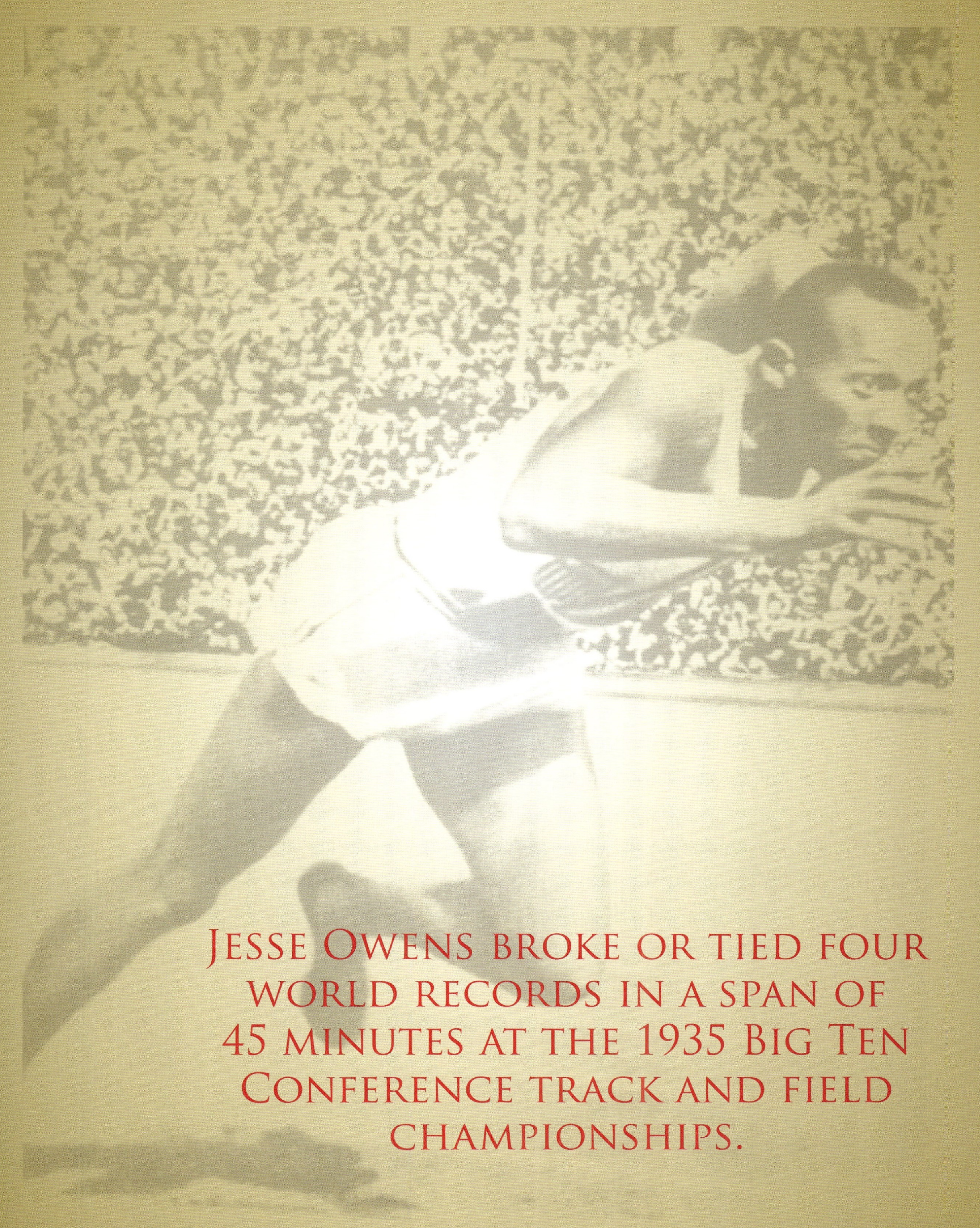

Jesse Owens broke or tied four world records in a span of 45 minutes at the 1935 Big Ten Conference track and field championships.

In 1972 Ohio State awarded Owens an honorary doctorate degree in athletic arts.

100 Years of African American Achievement at The Ohio State University

Keith B. Key's journey to success began in Pittsburgh as a Public Housing Kid with a dream and then later at The Ohio State University as a student athlete with a commitment to leadership.

Today Keith is the founder and CEO of KBK Enterprises, a real estate development firm whose mission is to "change lives" by going "beyond bricks and sticks." KBK Enterprises was established to provide real estate services in specific urban markets throughout the United States. KBK Enterprises has secured development contracts in Pittsburgh, PA, Washington DC, Chicago, IL, New York, NY, New Orleans, LA and throughout Ohio.

KBK Enterprises' President and CEO, Keith B. Key, has completed real estate development projects ranging from single and multifamily housing to commercial office facilities. KBK Enterprises has established significant relationships with churches and other faith based organizations, banks and governmental offices; to establish the necessary links to support the creation of one of the nation's largest African American real estate development firms.

DEVELOPMENT

CONSTRUCTION

PROPERTY MANAGEMENT

At KBK Enterprises....We Get It Done!

www.*kbkenterprises.net*

Prior to joining Fisher, Dumas was a visiting assistant professor at Goizueta Business School at Emory University and an assistant professor of organizational sciences at George Washington University.

Her primary research interests focus on how individuals can handle multiple role responsibilities and identities most effectively, and how companies can help their employees excel at work while also engaging meaningfully in their communities.

Currently, Dumas is researching the boundary between people's personal and professional lives. She is exploring assumptions of the so-called "ideal worker" — the image of the dedicated "company man" that was idealized in the 1950s. The married man with a stay-at-home wife remains a dominant image of an ideal worker in organizations; however, the single, childless worker also has emerged as an additional family configuration expected to live up to the ideal worker norm.

Dumas was a nominee for the Best Paper Award in the Organizational Behavior Division, Academy of Management in 2007, and a Top 20 Nominee for the Rosabeth Moss Kanter Award for Excellence in Work Family Research in 2006.

Before entering academia, Dumas conducted workforce-related research for a Chicago-based research and consulting firm.

David E. Harrison
Director
Office of Minority Student Services
June 1993-Present

David E. Harrison is director of the Office of Minority Student Services within the Max M. Fisher College of Business at The Ohio State University. Prior to serving in this role, he was an assistant director of recruitment and development and office manager within the Office of Minority Affairs at The Ohio State University. He joined the Office of Minority Affairs staff in 1987 as a recruiter/counselor and coordinator of the Minority Scholars Program.

Harrison received a Bachelor of Arts in political science at North Carolina A&T State University in 1985 and his Master of Arts in political science with an emphasis in public policy and theory at The Ohio State University in 1988. He received two Certificates of Commendations and an Honorable Discharge because of his service as a Reservist in the United States Marine Corps. He served for eight years (1985-1993) in the USMCR.

Harrison is a member of the Alpha Phi Alpha Fraternity, Inc. He is also a lifetime member of the NABA, NBMBAA, ALPFA, and the NSHMBAs. He is a 2004 inductee into the National Honor Society of Phi Kappa Phi. He is a past president of the NBMBAA-Columbus Chapter. He was recognized by that 7,000-member national organization in 2005 as its "NBMBAA National Member of the Year." He is currently featured as one of the most influential blacks in Columbus, in *Who's Who In Black Columbus,* 2010 Edition.

Lorraine Pennyman
Academic Counselor
Undergraduate Programs and Advising Office
May 2003-Present

Lorraine Pennyman is an academic counselor in the Undergraduate Programs and Advising Office. She holds a Masters in Education from the University of Cincinnati and received her undergraduate degree from Miami University (OH). Lorraine joined Fisher College of Business in 2003.

Lorraine academically advises, mentors and is a consistent source of support, motivation and guidance throughout a student's college career. In 2007, Lorraine became program coordinator of the Business Scholars Program, which she assisted in developing and implementing. The Business Scholars Program is one of 14 university scholars program that focuses on 50 incoming first-year students, providing them over a two-year span a supportive community, professional development and leadership opportunities early in their college career. Lorraine also coordinates the Fisher Alumni Mentorship Program (FAMP) which partners Fisher College of Business alumni with sophomore business students to enhance and develop professional meaningful relationships in their chosen business field.

Lorraine has presented at several conferences including the 2011 Ohio State Advising Conference. At the college level she has served on the Staff Advisory Committee and on the university level is constantly active with the Academic Advising Association at The Ohio State University (ACADAOS). In 2006, she was nominated for ACADAOS Advisor of the Year. Lorraine is currently president of ACADAOS.

Representative Diversity and Inclusion Activities

Recognition for Minority Recruitment and Retention
The recruitment and retention of African-American students is a priority of the college. In 1999, Fisher College of Business received recognition by the National Black MBA Association (NBMBAA) as the **Most Outstanding Educational Institution of the Year**. This distinguished award, which has been given out for more than 30 years, annually recognizes the educational institution that demonstrates outstanding achievement in the areas of student support and opportunities, enrollment in African-American student programs, diversity among faculty, sponsorship and support of NBMBAA initiatives and programs.

Most Outstanding Institution of the Year Award, September, 1999

Ohio State and Fisher were also ranked in the top two by *The Black EOE Journal* (2001) and the *Journal of Blacks in Higher Education (2003)* for the percentage of African-American students enrolled in its MBA program. In a 2004 report completed by the *Journal of Blacks in Higher Education,* Fisher College of Business was recognized as the only top-ranked business school with African-American students representing at least ten percent of its enrollment population.

Number One Ph.D. Producer
From 1994-2004, Fisher College of Business was arguably the United States' "Number One" producer of black Ph.D. students in business management. During that ten-year time frame, the Fisher produced 13 African-American Ph.D. graduates in business. Very few, if any, accredited business schools in the country can boast of such success. This success was due in part to a generous gift from the General Electric (GE) Faculty for the Future Foundation's grant.

Minority Assistantships, Scholarships, and Grants
Each year, the Office of Minority Student Services obtains funding from corporations and alumni to support graduate and undergraduate minority business students. In 2009, over $125,000 in scholarships, grants, and assistantships were awarded in support of minority students thanks to financial support from sponsors such as American Electric Power, Ernst & Young, Limited Brands, Shell, Exxon Mobil and KeyBank, among others. Corporate endowments, such as the PNC Minority Endowment Fund, provide additional income in the form of minority undergraduate scholarships each year.

Young Scholars Program
The Ohio State University Office of Diversity and Inclusion Young Scholars Program, (YSP) is a comprehensive pre-collegiate and collegiate program designed to enhance the academic, personal, and career development of its scholars. Founded in 1988, YSP annually identifies and serves hundreds of academically talented first-generation college students from economically challenged backgrounds.

In particular, YSP seeks:

- To enhance the academic preparation of scholars for success at The Ohio State University.
- To increase the numbers of first-generation, low-income targeted underrepresented students at The Ohio State University.
- To complement instruction offered during the academic year.

Each year, Fisher College of Business welcomes about 20 rising high school seniors who are interested in exploring a business degree. College faculty, students, and staff serve as guest speakers and provide a variety of career exploration activities and projects. These include introductions to the business academic disciplines from leading faculty, an introduction to career management, action-learning through business cases, and visits to local businesses.

Accounting Career Awareness Program (ACAP)
ACAP-OHIO is an innovative career development program designed specifically for minority high school students. This weeklong summer residency program was developed to give minority students an opportunity to explore careers in accounting and business.

During their stay on campus, students attend a variety of business and college preparatory workshops and are introduced to topics such as accounting, finance, economics, computer technology, and business management. ACAP is sponsored by the National Association of Black Accountants (NABA) and the Ohio Society of CPAs in conjunction with Fisher College of Business, which has hosted the program since 1998.

Some of the Young Scholars at Fisher College of Business, July, 2010

ACAP is a fully supervised, all-expenses-paid program backed with donations from leading businesses. Students selected for ACAP-Ohio will receive free tuition, room and board, books, materials, tours, and mentoring. ACAP has successfully impacted program participants, who overwhelmingly choose to pursue business and accounting majors upon entering college. A 1999 survey of past participants revealed that 43% of respondents have chosen college majors in accounting and 20% plan to major in business or finance.

Student and Professional Organization Membership and Conference Support
Since 1993, more than 240 graduate and undergraduate business students have received full financial support to attend National Black MBA Association (NBMBAA) conferences.

More impressively, Ohio State's Fisher College of Business has paid the student membership registration fee of **every** African-American PhD, MBA and Master's of Labor and Human Resources graduate student interested in being a member of NMBAA. More than 245 students have received two-year membership funding support from Ohio State. Similar support is provided for students who would like to become members of the National Association of Black Accountants.

Council of Black Students in Administration (CBSA): Almost 40 years and still standing...
The college is excited to note that it currently has more than 50 graduate and undergraduate business student organizations. Twelve of those organizations currently receive conference attendance funding support from the Office of Minority Student Services. The Council of Black Students in Administration (CBSA) is the oldest of those 12 minority business student organizations, with a rich history that dates back to its inception in 1972.

It was founded, after and in response to the nation's civil rights struggles of the 1960s, with the objective and purpose of facilitating and promoting strength, communications, and unity between the African-American students interested in the administrative sciences. To this day, it continues to persevere and stands as a vehicle for aiding its members in academic, professional, community outreach, and social development. Its founding members include Jim Austin, who served as its first president, and Norwood Thomas, who served as its fourth president. Its advisors over the years have included Jermaine Simpson, Deborah Bibb, David Harrison and Danielle Brown.

OSU's NBMBAA Conference Case Competition Finalist Team with OSU Professor Marc Ankerman (Coach), NBMBAA Interim President and CEO Steve Lewis, and the Case Competition Sponsor's Chrysler Corporate Executives. Los Angeles, Calif. September, 2010

KeyBank Minority MBA Case Competition and Undergraduate Creativity and Leadership Symposium
KeyBank has been a strong supporter of the Office of Minority Student Services at Fisher.

KeyBank Undergraduate Creativity and Leadership Symposium Scholarship recipients October, 2010

KeyBank's relationship with Fisher and Ohio State has resulted in the creation of two of the office's leading programs for minority students at the graduate and undergraduate levels.

The KeyBank Minority MBA Case Competition began in 2005 and attracts 16-20 teams of MBA students from around the country to participate in the nationally recognized MBA student case competition at the KeyBank headquarters in Cleveland, Ohio. Each year, over $15,000 is awarded in prizes to the top four teams. KeyBank's support of the minority case competition also includes financial assistance to one or two graduate assistants who help make the program a success.

In 2007, KeyBank expanded its support of the college to include an undergraduate minority business student initiative: the **Undergraduate Creativity and Leadership Symposium.**

This event brings together undergraduate students from around the country and offers a unique educational experience that builds upon the traditional business management education coursework. The annual symposium provides underrepresented business junior and senior students a three-day intensive program on leadership, unleashing creativity, product innovation, entrepreneurial thinking, persuasive communication, professional development, and the art of "putting it all together." To date, three symposiums have been held and 106 students from schools across the country have participated in the event held on the Fisher College of Business campus.

National Black MBA Association (NBMBAA) Leadership
At least eight Ohio State alumni have served throughout the United States as NBMBAA chapter presidents (Carey Cheri, Leslie Epps, Myron Hoskins, Deborah Bibb, Vanessa Enoch, Eric Lenard, David Harrison and Buffie Patterson).

NBMBAA Member of the Year, David Harrison (center), with Ohio State students and Oyaauma Garrison (past president of the Columbus chapter) at the NBMBAA Conference in San Diego September, 2005

KeyBank Undergraduate Creativity and Leadership Symposium Participants, October, 2010

Richard Thomas and Terina Matthews, Alumni Awards Program, May, 2007

Anslee Johnson with Ami Scott, Fisher College of Business Diversity Awards Recipient, May, 2004

Fisher College of Business Diversity Awards Program, Reception and Alumni Reunion

The Fisher College of Business Diversity Awards Program was created to recognize those individuals and corporations who have made significant contributions in advancing the college's diversity efforts. Each year, one individual and one corporation are recognized at the awards program and reception. Past diversity awards winners are invited to attend the event as well.

Some previous individual award winners include: Kamran Jameel, Terina Matthews, Ming Shiao, Christina Ballenger, Lawrence Funderburke, Adiya Mittal, Ami Scott, Marci Chambers, and Eric Lenard. Previous corporate award recipients include Nationwide Insurance Company, Ashland, Inc., LimitedBrands, Procter & Gamble, Ernst & Young, KeyBank, Ross Products, INROADS, and PNC (formerly National City Bank).

Dana Washington, Jackie Kemp and Sameer Bagga with Lawrence Funderburke, Fisher College of Business Diversity Awards Recipient, May 2006

Special Tribute to

Frank W. Hale, Jr., Ph.D.

By Adam King, on Campus Staff

Ohio State Professor Emeritus Frank Hale Jr. was among the 250,000 people in Washington, DC, in 1963 who stood transfixed as Martin Luther King Jr. stepped in front of the Lincoln Memorial and delivered his "I Have a Dream" speech.

A picture framing that moment hangs on Hale's wall — a constant reminder that treating one's fellow humans with dignity and respect can overcome misunderstanding and hatred. And yet, as Hale recounted his life in advance of his 84th year and being inducted into the Ohio Civil Rights Hall of Fame, which he was on October 14, 2010, it was a much smaller moment that brought the beginning of tears to his eyes.

Hale's fourth-grade teacher, Luvada Lockhart, was "the spark" that lit his mental fire, leading him to a life worth remembering. In a single room adjacent to a church in Missouri, Lockhart taught 60 children in grades 1-8, "but she made us all feel important," said Hale. He had struggled in the second and third grades as one of only three black kids in a mostly white school in Campbell, Ohio, while living with his aunt while his mother was ill.

"Luvada used to pat me on the shoulder and say, 'Son, you can do it,'" Hale said. "She walked around the room and never sat. She was always attending to the individual needs of students."

Hale never lost his newfound self-esteem after that, even when confronted with the daily injustices African Americans faced in the South while living in Kansas, Missouri and Alabama — separate drinking fountains and toilets, separate waiting rooms at the bus station and even separate basketball teams in the same high school.

That single year spent with Lockhart also showed him how profound an effect one person can have on the life of another.

"When I think of Luvada Lockhart, I'm reminded of my obligation," Hale said.

Hale dedicated his life to his own education and teaching others — a quality instilled by his father, who would leave books on black history for Hale to read during the summers, and they would discuss the books when his father returned home from work.

Hale skipped three grades starting with the fifth grade because of his advanced knowledge and attended Oakwood College (now Oakwood University) in Huntsville, Ala., at age 16 (after turning down a four-year scholarship to Howard University at age 15).

He finished his undergraduate and master's degrees at the University of Nebraska and went on to earn his doctorate from Ohio State in 1955 in communications and political science.

By then Hale's desire to see racial equality had taken root. His first teaching position was at Oakwood in 1951, and he made it a point to give students a first-hand look at history in the making. In December 1955, Hale took three carloads of students almost 200 miles to see Rosa Parks' Montgomery bus trial, which sparked a year-long city bus boycott led by King that ended rider segregation.

"I never considered myself to be an angry young man," said Hale, "but I always considered myself to be an aware young man. My father had kept me abreast of great writers and speakers during the Harlem Renaissance movement: Countee Cullen, Langston Hughes, Arna Bontemps, David Walker, Frederick Douglass — people in spite of their surroundings and condition had really made a name for themselves and contributed as leaders to that movement in America. So I was an activist as a teacher, and I was very much concerned that black kids recognized their history. Without their history, they would be defenseless."

In 1959 Hale became chair of the Department of English at Central State University in Wilberforce before leaving for the presidency of Oakwood College in 1966. He was offered a second five-year term, but turned it down when OSU came calling.

One of the black students he met during his interview process at Ohio State broke down in tears, telling him if he didn't go back to Oakwood, "'that college would still have faculty and staff of color there, but we don't have anybody here,'" Hale recalled. "That struck a chord. Black students at Ohio State were living in a sea of whiteness."

Once he agreed to come, it didn't take long for Hale to make an imprint.

He turned Ohio State into the nation's top producer of African-American PhDs by the end of the 1970s by instituting the Graduate and Professional Students Visitation Days program three months after his arrival in 1971.

Frank W. Hale, Jr. and U.S. Secretary of Commerce Ron Brown

Using his experience as a United Negro College Fund board of trustees member, Hale invited about 300 seniors with 3.0 grade-point averages or better from historically black colleges to Ohio State each November and showed them how the university was committed to their success. It was an outreach effort backed up by $15 million Hale had secured from the administration to offer aid to those students who chose to complete their graduate studies as Buckeyes.

"People in my generation, anybody who had master's or PhD degrees did not get them in the South," Hale said. "So I didn't think I was taking a risk asking these black college presidents to send us their best black students. It worked like hotcakes."

Hale also was instrumental in working with the Department of Black Studies (now African American and African Studies) and the administration to create a Black Cultural Center on campus, which had been in limbo for a decade. The renovated Bradford Commons was designed to be a hub of education for students of different ethnicities where they could learn how various cultures enriched western and global civilization.

In honor of Hale's work to secure the center and his service to the university, it was named for him upon its official opening in 1989.

"THESE PROGRAMS ARE WORKING, AND THAT'S WHY I CALL MYSELF AN ACADEMIC ACTIVIST."

It is the only building on campus named for an African American other than Jesse Owens.

"It's nice to smell your flowers before you're outta here," Hale said.

Hale started the Minority Scholars Program in 1982 and had 500 students go through the program before he retired in 1988. The program still exists today.

Frank W. Hale, Jr. and Julian Bond

"These programs are working, and that's why I call myself an academic activist," Hale said. "I've been so excited about the possibility of teaching young people and motivating them to recognize what their potential is. Basically teaching is a touch of immortality in motivating a child to be the best he can be and you live on in them. That's the best reward you can get."

Hale returned to Ohio State in 1999 and remained until 2005 as Distinguished University Representative and Consultant in the office of the president under William Kirwan and then Karen Holbrook. Kirwan had asked Hale to start a minority recruitment program at the University of Maryland when Kirwan was provost there before becoming Maryland's and then OSU's president.

Frank W. Hale, Jr. and Rev. Jessie Jackson

Once out of retirement, Hale started the President and Provost's Lecture and Cultural Arts Series, bringing in outstanding minority scholars and artists to speak at OSU. That legacy continues today as the President and Provost's Diversity Lecture Series.

Hale said being able to attend his Ohio Civil Rights Hall of Fame induction at age 83 was a special moment.

"My career has been a very rich one, a very fulfilling one," Hale said. "I'm just so happy the Ohio Civil Rights Commission is doing this because I think people forget how powerful those two words are: civil rights. To be civil, to me, is to be polite, to be courteous, be chivalrous, with a note of gallantry and nobility in all of that. I don't know how you can be civil and be intolerant too or civil and be bigoted and mean or menacing. I sense a lot in the atmosphere right now that is challenging that concept."

Hale Hall
Frank W. Hale, Jr.
Black Cultural Center
153 West 12th Avenue
Hale Hall

The Kirwan Institute for the Study of Race and Ethnicity

Executive Director john a. powell

The Kirwan Institute for the Study of Race and Ethnicity is a university-wide, interdisciplinary research institute that works to deepen understanding of the causes of – and solutions to – racial and ethnic disparities worldwide and to bring about a society that is fair and just for all people.

Kirwan Institute research is designed to be actively used to solve problems in society. Its research and staff expertise are shared through an extensive network of colleagues and partners – ranging from other researchers to on-the-ground social justice advocates, policymakers, and community leaders nationally and globally, who can quickly put ideas into action.

The Kirwan Institute's History and Inception

The Kirwan Institute for the Study of Race and Ethnicity was established at The Ohio State University in May of 2003 in a combined effort between the College of Humanities, the Moritz College of Law and The College of Social and Behavioral Sciences. Its initial focus was to:

- Foster critical and creative thinking on concepts about race and ethnicity;
- Examine hierarchies and systems of control, domination, and oppression;
- Explore the interrelatedness of race and ethnicity to other foci such as gender and class;
- Examine the cultural, economic, political, and social experiences of racial and ethnic minority groups in the Americas; and to
- Interrogate the material conditions of life and achievement among groups who are systematically subjected to systems of domination and oppression.

The Institute is named for William E. "Brit" Kirwan, former President of The Ohio State University, in recognition of his significant and successful efforts to champion diversity at the University. Since leaving Ohio State in 2002, former President Kirwan has continued to support the Institute.

World-Class Leadership

The Institute is led by Executive Director john a. powell, an internationally recognized authority in the areas of civil rights, civil liberties, and issues related to race, ethnicity, poverty and the law. powell also holds the Williams Chair in Civil Rights & Civil Liberties at the Moritz College of Law at The Ohio State University.

Deputy Director Andrew Grant-Thomas is a national leader on issues related to race, ethnicity, poverty, structural racism/racialization, and implicit bias. He speaks and writes frequently on these issues and on popular cultural references to race and ethnicity.

Both leaders are often quoted in the national media.

Deputy Director
Andrew Grant-Thomas

Kirwan Institute Research

The Kirwan Institute's research supports the notion that all communities of people are interconnected and society benefits when all human capabilities are developed and maximized to serve the greater good. Its research is focused in five key areas:

Structural Racialization and Systems Thinking examines how systems and system components are arranged and structured to distribute social meaning, identity, benefits, and burdens in particular situations and how these structures can be modified and transformed.

The Opportunity Communities Program identifies, and works to understand and eliminate, racialized structural barriers to opportunity in critical domains including education, housing, employment, health and health care, and civic engagement, in order to build opportunity-rich neighborhoods and communities.

Talking About Race examines how the form and content of communications influence the way in which racialized messages are received and processed; and this initiative works to create communications messages and strategies that highlight our linked fates.

Race in the Mind examines the processes by which attitudes and ideas about race help shape the relationship between race and opportunity and how the harmful effects can be mitigated.

The Global Justice Program examines how racialized structures contribute to enormous political, social and economic disparities that marginalize billions of people in our global society, and explores how these inequities can be alleviated.

Kirwan Institute Work

The Kirwan Institute's research shows that structural barriers within society sometimes prevent people from accessing opportunity. Such barriers are not always obvious to others – yet they can be very real obstacles to success. Sustainable jobs, quality education, safe and affordable housing, a healthy environment, and access to health care are all important factors for stability and personal advancement in life. These factors and others interact to create a "web of opportunity." How people and groups are situated within the "web" significantly influences their chances for happiness and success in life.

The Kirwan Institute uses a structural/systems approach to investigate the cause and consequences of racial disparities and to conceive policy solutions. Here are a few examples of specific projects.

Vacant Property in Detroit, Michigan

In a city inundated with tens of thousands of vacant properties, advocates in the Detroit region have long pushed for a land bank program to redevelop vacant land and revitalize neighborhoods. Working with MOSES (a Gamaliel chapter in Detroit), the Institute provided extensive assistance to aid the land bank advocacy efforts in the Detroit region. After several years of extensive effort by advocacy organizations, both Wayne County, Michigan, and the City of Detroit have created new land bank programs. These new programs come at a critical juncture in Detroit's history, with vacant property challenges escalating due to the foreclosure crisis.

Austin, Texas, Opportunity Initiative; Affordable Housing

Working with the housing advocacy organization Green Doors in Austin, Texas, the Institute completed an opportunity mapping assessment of the Austin region. Since the completion of this work, advocates across Austin have utilized the opportunity maps to inform decisions. Recently, the City of Austin's affordable housing development programs utilized the Institute's opportunity maps to assess affordable housing investments in the city.

Thompson v. HUD and Fair Housing in Baltimore

Working with the NAACP Legal Defense Fund and the Maryland ACLU on behalf of more than 15,000 public housing residents represented in a class action lawsuit, the Institute has helped design a remedial fair housing strategy for the Baltimore region. The Institute's opportunity mapping and opportunity-based housing model was utilized to design a 7,000 housing unit fair housing program in response to a Fair Housing Act violation found against the U.S. Department of Housing and Urban Development. The U.S. District Court Judge's final ruling on the proposed remedy is expected soon.

Student Assignment Planning for Montclair, New Jersey

All school districts that utilized race-based school assignment plans are potentially impacted by the Parents Involved Supreme Court decision which placed limits on school districts' options for voluntary school integration. The Kirwan Institute has worked with several school districts to review, assess, and design different strategies for producing sustainable, diverse and successful schools. In New Jersey, the Montclair district utilized the model proposed by the Institute in the redesign of its magnet school-based student attendance policy, utilizing school performance, poverty and race in its new student assignment plan.

Neighborhood Revitalization in Columbus, Ohio

Working as a consultant to the Columbus Foundation, the Institute helped to design a neighborhood revitalization strategy for Columbus, Ohio. In addition, the strategies and recommendations produced by the Institute have informed the local United Way's effort to redesign its neighborhood revitalization program. Ideally, these two initiatives will direct significant funds into neighborhood revitalization for marginalized Columbus-area communities.

Equitable Regionalism in Cleveland, Ohio

The Institute worked on behalf of African-American political and business leaders in the Cleveland region to develop a plan for equitable regionalism in Northeast Ohio. Several of the strategy and policy recommendations posed in this work have been adopted in the region. These include creation of a new regional magnet school in the city of Cleveland, a minority business accelerator for the region, and a regionalism cabinet position in the City of Cleveland.

In addition to the policies suggested by the Institute, the Institute also helped strengthen the engagement of African-American leaders around the issues of regionalism, regional development and revenue sharing in Northeast Ohio.

Franklin County, Ohio, Housing Trust Fund

Working with BREAD (Building Responsibility Equity and Dignity), the Institute conducted research to illustrate areas of extreme housing need in Columbus, Ohio. The research was utilized to fuel an advocacy campaign which succeeded in expanding funding for extremely low-income households through the Franklin County Housing Trust Fund.

Input on Human Rights to a United Nations Committee

In collaboration with more than 250 civic groups and scholars, the Kirwan Institute contributed to a report presented to the United Nations Committee on the Elimination of Racial Discrimination (CERD). The report, The Structural Racism Report to the CERD Committee, documents and explains how institutional policies and practices in the United States contribute to the production of racial inequity, even in the absence of racist actors or malicious intent. The Kirwan Institute's language is prominently featured throughout the report's executive summary, becoming part of the "official record" of the committee's work.

Kirwan Institute Mission

The Kirwan Institute partners with people, communities, and institutions worldwide to think about, talk about, and act on race in ways that create and expand opportunity for all.

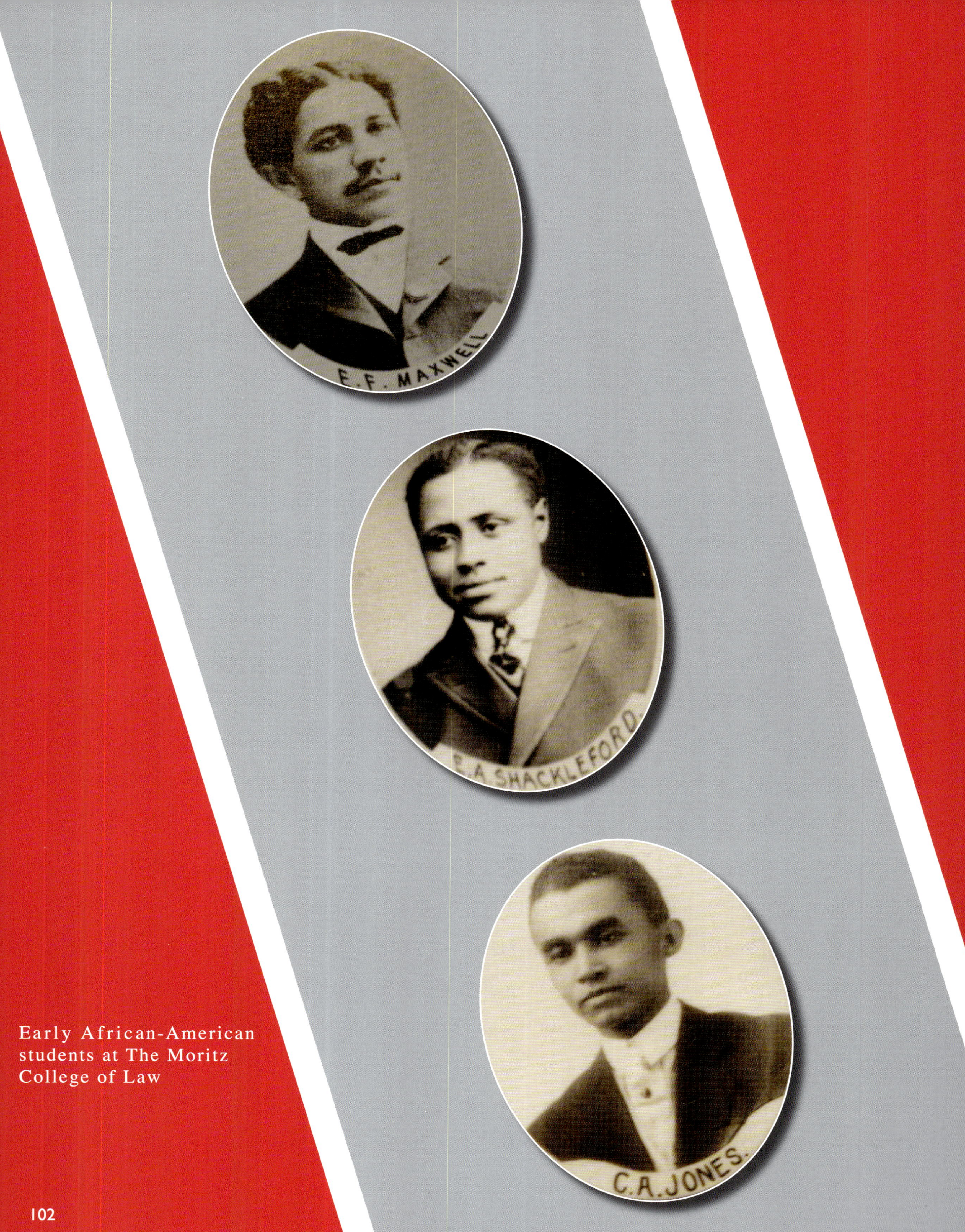

Early African-American students at The Moritz College of Law

THE MORITZ COLLEGE OF LAW

The Moritz College of Law was established in 1891. It was a charter member of the American Association of Law Schools, which along with the American Bar Association (ABA), is the governing body for all ABA accredited law schools in the United States and Canada.

Robert Soloman, Assistant Dean for Admissions and Director of Minority Affairs

The Trailblazers

The earliest record of African Americans being enrolled at the Moritz College of Law is 1903. Earl Frederick Maxwell of Xenia, Ohio, was a student, but not listed as a graduate. In 1906 Elmer Amos Shackelford of Tipton, Missouri, graduated with a Certificate in Law at the 29th Annual Commencement ceremony. In 1911 William Otis Stokes of Dayton, Ohio, was also awarded a Certificate in Law. He was noted to be a member of Alpha Phi Alpha Fraternity, Inc. and the Hunter Law Society.

The first official African-American graduate of The Ohio State University College of Law was Clarence Alexander Jones, a native of West Virginia. A member of the class of 1912, he was also a member of the debating team, the Debate and Oratory Council, Alpha Phi Alpha Fraternity, Inc. and the Hunter Law Society. The 1912 yearbook referred to Jones as, "A worthy representative of his race and a diligent student of the law." Jones received a Bachelor of Arts degree from Ohio State in 1910 and his LLB (the equivalent to the juris doctorate degree today) in 1912. He was admitted to the California Bar in 1913, where he had a successful legal career until he passed away in 1948. Although Jones moved away to practice law in California, the legacy of Ohio State remained within his family. His great grandson, Loren Simmons, is a member of the class of 2012 and will graduate 100 years after his great grandfather.

Loren Simmons

The first African-American woman to graduate from the College of Law was Eva Mae Parker Crosby of Selma, Alabama. Crosby attended high school in Oberlin, Ohio, where she graduated in 1929. She went on to matriculate at Oberlin College and graduated in 1933. In 1936 she received her law degree from The Ohio State University College of Law. She returned to Oberlin after law school, becoming a house developer, teacher, community activist and attorney. Crosby moved back to Columbus in 1963, taught at Roosevelt Junior High School and became a successful entrepreneur, running Crosby Funeral Home from the death of her husband in 1966 until she passed away in 2002.

Trailblazers such as Clarence Jones and Eva Crosby paved the way for hundreds of African-American lawyers who have become trendsetters today.

The Trendsetters

There are a myriad of successful African-American lawyers who once graced the halls of the Moritz College of Law. They have all become trendsetters in their own right. Only a few notable alums are featured in this section:

The Bench

The Honorable Yvette McGee Brown and family

The Honorable Yvette McGee Brown '85 earned her bachelor's degree from Ohio University. She has served as an Assistant Attorney General for Ohio and a Judge in the Franklin County Court of Common Pleas. In 2011 she became the first African-American woman Justice on the Supreme Court of Ohio.

The Honorable Robert M. Duncan '52, a native of Urbana, Ohio, earned both his Bachelor of Science and juris doctorate degrees from OSU. His judicial career began when he became a Judge in the Franklin County Municipal Court. In 1969 he was elected to the Ohio Supreme Court where he served until his appointment as Judge of the U.S. Court of Military Appeals in 1971. In 1974 he was named Chief Justice of this court. Shortly thereafter, he was appointed to the U.S. District Court for the Southern District of Ohio.

The Honorable Robert M. Duncan, retired Ohio Surpreme Court Justice

It was in this position that Duncan wrote the landmark order ending segregation in the Columbus Public Schools. His fairness, leadership, and accessibility to community groups helped ensure a smooth process of desegregation. He was often the first African American to hold many of his posts throughout his illustrious career.

The Honorable Donald L. Graham

The Honorable Donald L. Graham '74 earned his bachelor's degree from West Virginia State College. Graham served on active duty in the U.S. Army, the JAG (Judge Advocate General) Corps, and in the United States Attorney's Office in the Southern District of Florida. In 1991 he was appointed to the United States District Court for the Southern District of Florida.

The Honorable Jeffrey P. Hopkins '85 earned his bachelor's degree from Bowdoin College. He has served as a Judicial Law Clerk, an associate in private practice and an Assistant United States Attorney. In 1996 he was appointed a U.S. Bankruptcy Judge in Cincinnati, Ohio.

The Honorable Judge Timothy Horton sworn in by Federal Judge Algenon L. Marbley

The Honorable Timothy Horton '95 earned his bachelor's degree from Boston University. He was elected Judge in 2006 to the Franklin County Common Pleas Court. He serves as a guest lecturer and speaker for the Moritz College of Law.

The Board Room

Michael E. Flowers
Chief Legal Officer of KBK Enterprises

Michael E. Flowers '79 earned his bachelor's degree from Bucknell University. He had a distinguished career in private law practice and became Chair of the American Bar Association Business Section. He now serves as Vice President and Chief Legal Officer of KBK Enterprises.

Stephen S. Francis
Manager of Diversity Relations,
Honda of America Mfg. Inc.

Stephen S. Francis '84 earned his bachelor's degree from Morehouse College. He has had a successful career in both the public and private sector before joining Honda of America Mfg. Inc. where he serves as Unit Manager of Diversity Relations.

Steve Jemison
Chief Legal Officer, Procter & Gamble

Steve Jemison '75 earned his bachelor's degree from Elmhurst College. He worked for the Federal Communications Commission and the National Labor Relations Board before joining Procter & Gamble, where he worked his way up to Chief Legal Officer in 2008.

Douglas L. Williams
Senior Vice President and General Counsel for Limited Brands, Inc.

Douglas L. Williams '80 earned his bachelor's degree from the U.S. Air Force Academy, and a master's degree from Central Missouri State University. He had a successful career in private law practice before assuming the helm as Senior Vice President and General Counsel for Limited Brands, Inc.

The Bar

Otto Beatty, Jr.
Distinguished Attorney at Law

Otto Beatty, Jr. '67 has served the Columbus community for several decades. In addition to private practice, he spent 18 years in the Ohio House of Representatives. His legal expertise in public policy has earned him a reputation as a powerful advocate for minority business development and disadvantaged citizens throughout the state of Ohio.

W. Ray Persons
Equity Partner, King & Spalding Law Firm

W. Ray Persons '78 earned his bachelor's degree from Armstrong State College. He is a nationally renowned trial lawyer who specializes in complex litigation, and lectures all over the country. He is an Equity Partner at the law firm of King & Spalding in Atlanta, Georgia.

Kathleen and Frederick Ransier
Partners, Vorys, Sater, Seymour and Pease LLP

Kathleen '74 & ***Frederick Ransier*** '74 have been the epitome of the successful husband/wife team in law practice. Kathy earned her bachelor's degree from Western College and has had a wide range of practice areas including commercial finance and corporate business. Fred earned his bachelor's degree from Central State University. His practice areas include among other things, bankruptcy and creditors' rights as well as litigation. Kathy and Fred successfully ran the Ransier & Ransier law firm for decades before merging with Vorys, Sater, Seymour and Pease LLP to become partners.

Carl D. Smallwood
Partner, Vorys, Sater, Seymour and Pease LLP

Carl D. Smallwood '80 earned both his bachelor's and juris doctorate degrees from OSU. He has had a flourishing career as a partner in the law firm of Vorys, Sater, Seymour and Pease LLP, focusing on labor and employment and litigation. Carl was also the first African-American President of the Columbus Bar Association.

Black Law Students Association 2006-2007

Linda Ammons
Dean of the Widener University School of Law

The Academy

Linda Ammons '87 earned her bachelor's degree from Oakwood College as well as a master's degree from OSU. She has had a distinguished career as a practicing lawyer working for former Ohio Governor Ted Celeste and as a law professor, first at Cleveland State University law school and currently as Dean of the Widener University School of Law. She was the first African-American woman to lead the Widener University law school.

John W. Garland '74 earned his bachelor's degree from Central State University, where he currently serves as President. He has been a prolific lawyer in government, private practice and in higher education, working as Associate Vice Provost at the University of Virginia before taking the helm at Central State University.

LeRoy Pernell '74 earned his bachelor's degree from Franklin & Marshall College. He has had a distinguished career as both a practicing lawyer and a law professor, serving as a professor in The Moritz College of Law, Vice Provost for Minority Affairs at OSU, Dean of the Northern Illinois University College of Law, and currently Dean of Florida A&M College of Law.

Black Law Students Association 2007-2008

Black Law Students Association 2008-2009

Black Law Students Association 2009-2010

Black Law Students Association 2010-2011

Shaping the Profession

The Moritz College of Law continues to develop more African-American law students to enter the profession. The law school has developed a rich legacy of diversity throughout the past 100 years. The law school had its first African-American Dean in the person of Gregory H. Williams in the early 1990s, who is currently President of the University of Cincinnati. Today The Moritz College of Law has seven African-American faculty, with three African Americans serving in senior administration.

Gregory H. Williams
President, University of Cincinnati

Michelle Alexander
Assoc. Professor of Law

Sharon Davies
John C. Elam/Vorys Sater Designated Professor of Law

Garry Jenkins
Assoc. Dean for Academic Affairs

Creola Johnson
Professor of Law

Kathy Northern
Assoc. Dean for Admissions
Associate Professor

john a. powell
Gregory H. Williams Chair in Civil Rights and Civil Liberties

Vincene Verdun
Assoc. Professor of Law

A Brief Historical Summary of Black Studies at OSU

By Professor James N. Upton and Carla Wilks 

The Black Studies Division was born out of the struggle and sacrifice of black students at The Ohio State University. Its origin dates back to the decision by black students in 1968 to unite around the issue of the need for fundamental changes in university policies affecting the lives of black people. Throughout its history, the University had enforced policies of institutional racism which kept black enrollment to a bare minimum and denied the few blacks enrolled equal opportunities in practically every aspect of campus life. One looked in vain for evidence of the tremendous contributions made by black Americans in the areas of music, art, politics, economics and many others in the University's course offerings. Not a single black professor was to be found in the entire College of Arts and Sciences; this dismal record was paralleled by the near total exclusion of blacks at the professorial level in most other colleges in the University. Segregation in campus social activities was rampant. White fraternities remained white; black fraternities remained black and largely unrecognized by University officials as legitimate student organizations. In general, the image presented by The Ohio State University to the black community was one of profound antipathy to black involvement, black creativity, black awareness, and black social and intellectual development.

The crucial stimulus for black student action designed to break down the prevailing system of institutional racism was a mass meeting featuring black activist Dick Gregory. In a ringing address, Gregory indicted the University for its lack of progress on the racial front, and urged black students to organize politically in defense of their rights as sovereign citizens in the University community. Within days of Gregory's appeal for black unity and action, the Black Student Union (BSU) was organized to spearhead the development of a vigorous black movement on campus.

As official representatives of OSU black students, BSU leaders began to vocalize black student dissatisfaction with University policies.

Receiving little response to their pleas for reform from University officials, BSU leaders decided to dramatize black student grievances through a sit-in demonstration at the Administration Building. This demonstration, taking place in April of 1968, resulted in the arrest of 34 black students on a variety of charges including trespassing, malicious destruction of public property and conspiracy to kidnap.

The April mass arrest virtually decimated the leadership element of the BSU. As a consequence, the effectiveness of the BSU as a campus protest organization began to rapidly diminish. Lacking a cohesive organizational base, the black movement on campus, which earlier had shown significant promise, began to unravel. By the end of the 1968 school year, black student unrest had practically disappeared from the arena of campus politics.

The black students' uprising of 1968, while short lived, was not without its visible results.

In the wake of the mass arrest of black students, University officials began, for the first time, to show a serious interest in addressing themselves to black concerns by launching a vigorous campaign to hire new black faculty for the 1969-70 school year. Additionally, the University committed itself to the establishment of a Black Studies Program, and sought to underscore this commitment with the appointment of a committee to make initial probes into the area of Black Studies and to advise the Provost regarding appropriate steps for implementing plans for establishing a Black Studies unit.

When school began in the fall of 1969, black students generally agreed that in spite of the conciliatory moves made by the University after the 1968 uprising, there was still a need for an effective black student protest organization. Consequently, they decided to form the Afro-American Society (Afro-Am) to pick up the mantle of leadership left vacant by the BSU in 1968. The leadership corps of Afro-Am represented a mixture of experienced black student leaders, and a younger group of dynamic black spokesmen entering into the mainstream of campus politics for the first time. Eventually, the latter group became the predominant and controlling force, with leaders of the defunct BSU engaging primarily in roles of policy initiation and implementation.

The Black Studies Division attained department status in 1972, at which time Dr. William E. Nelson Jr., was named Chair of the department.

The founding of Afro-Am was accompanied by the appointment of a new Black Studies Committee. This group was charged with the responsibility of conducting a wide-ranging search for a Black Studies Director, and in the interim, laying the foundation for the inauguration of a Black Studies Program during the fall quarter of the 1970-71 school year. After nearly eight months of vigorous activity, the Black Studies Committee recommended to the provost that Charles O. Ross, a University of Chicago faculty member and long-time community organizer, be hired as director of the Black Studies Division. The committee's recommendation was accepted by the University administration but rejected by the board of trustees. Subsequent maneuvering by faculty and student groups resulted in reconsideration by the board of the Ross appointment and a reversal of its initial decision.

The Black Studies Division began operating as a unit of the College of Humanities in July of 1969. From the beginning, the Division became involved in a political conflict between a determined Chair and a generally resistant University bureaucracy. Year-long disagreements over budgets, administrative authority and relations, philosophy, and the extension of the Division's functions to the non-university black population culminated in a decision by University officials in June of 1971, not to recommend Charles Ross' reappointment for another year as Black Studies Director. This decision was ratified by the board of trustees in July of 1971. Although removed from his Black Studies post, Ross retained his position as a tenured faculty member in the School of Social Work. Subsequent to Ross' dismissal, administrative matters in the Black Studies Division were coordinated by Dr. William E. Nelson Jr., who served in the capacity of Acting Director.

Despite major obstacles, the Black Studies Division was remarkably successful in accomplishing many of its most important first-year goals. The Division served as a home and a rallying point for black students seeking assistance and reinforcement of group identification. The Director of the Division served as an adviser to numerous black students' organizations and was instrumental in the formation of the Black Choir, Proud Black Images, the United Black Faculty and Staff Organization, and the Black Education Center. Eight full-time faculty members were added to the staff of the Black Studies Division. More than 20 courses were introduced into the University's curriculum, with a number of others in various stages of preparation. An undergraduate major in Black Studies was established, and plans for offering courses at the graduate level were initiated, resulting in the establishment of the Master of Arts program in 1975.

The Black Studies Division attained department status in 1972, at which time Dr. William E. Nelson Jr., was named Chair of the department. Also in 1972, through the efforts of personnel in the Department of Black Studies and the Division of Continuing Education, the Community Extension Center was established. In 1993, the department's name was changed from the Department of Black Studies to the African American and African Studies Department.

Esteemed
Alumni

Canise Y. Bean, D.M.D., MPH
Associate Professor - Clinical
Director of Community Education
The Ohio State University College of Dentistry

Class of 1995

Dr. Canise Bean matriculated at Texas Southern University, in Houston, Texas, majoring in pre-dentistry. She returned to Lexington, Kentucky, to attend dental school at the University of Kentucky College of Dentistry. Upon attaining her Doctor of Dentistry Medicine degree, she moved to Cleveland, Ohio, where she completed a general practice residency at Cleveland Metropolitan General Hospital. Bean then became a founding member of Shaker Dental Associates, the first African-American private dental group practice. Fulfilling a desire to impart knowledge to others, she was a part-time faculty member at Case Western Reserve University Dental School. She was also an instructor at Shaker Dental Institute, a dental assisting training program managed by Shaker Dental Associates and the first of its kind to be state certified. Bean was elected to serve as the first female president of Forest City Dental Society, an organization comprised of 60 minority dentists in the Cleveland area.

Bean relocated to Columbus and received a Master of Public Health degree from The Ohio State University (OSU). She was in private practice for five years before joining the faculty at OSU in the Section of Restorative and Prosthetic Dentistry. Her duties included instruction in preclinical courses and student supervision in the clinic. She received a Student Government Award and was recognized as an Outstanding Teacher by the Class of 2002.

Bean currently directs the major outreach program for the College, the OHIO (Oral Health Improvement through Outreach) Project, which is the pipeline program previously funded by the Robert Wood Johnson Foundation. The OHIO Project has changed clinical dental education so that students spend 50 days of their clinical education in community-based sites, thereby addressing the number one unmet health care need in the state — access to oral health care.

Bean is a life member of Delta Sigma Theta Sorority, Inc. and the Twin Rivers Chapter of The Links, Incorporated. She is married to the Reverend Dr. Michael R. Bean Sr., pastor of St. Paul A.M.E. Church, and is the mother of Michael Jr. and Yvette.

Otto Beatty Jr.
Attorney at Law
Otto Beatty Jr. & Associates, LPA

Class of 1967

Otto Beatty Jr. learned the value of hard work working at his father's restaurant on the Near East Side of Columbus, Ohio. Beatty met lawyers dining there and was inspired by their legal accomplishments, commitment to community activities, and efforts to share and change public policy.

That early exposure guided him as he became one of the gifted students who enrolled in University High School on the campus of The Ohio State University. The teenage Beatty was introduced to Ohio State's College of Law during study sessions in the law library. He went on to attend and graduate from Howard University during the height of the civil rights movement, where Beatty observed lawyers at the forefront of civil rights and business leadership.

Beatty played professional football with the Denver Broncos. When that ended, he returned to Columbus to attend law school at Ohio State. His years there represented a part of the school's history; he was the only African-American student in his law school class, and for a while, the only black student in the entire program. Beatty graduated with both a law degree and an MBA. After a two-year tenure with the Columbus Legal Aid Society, he established one of the largest and most revered minority law firms in central Ohio.

His career includes several significant firsts, including becoming the first African-American lawyer to own a law building in downtown Columbus. That building housed dozens of lawyers, including two prominent Ohio State law graduates: Leroy Pernell, the first African-American full-time law professor, and John Bowen, the first black Ohio Senator from Columbus. He argued before the Ohio Supreme Court on such landmark decisions as the constitutional right to have bail in Ohio, published numerous articles in legal journals, and lectured for the Ohio State Bar and forums across the United States, the Caribbean, South Africa and Taiwan. He also served as president of the Franklin County Lawyers Association.

Beatty used his legal expertise to affect public policy during a storied two-decade career in the Ohio House of Representatives. He gained national attention as the author of legislation for minority business development and performing Columbus' first disparity study that showed that, before this legislation, minorities could only obtain less than one-half of one percent of state contracts for construction and goods and services.

John W.E. Bowen III
Former State Senator
Class of 1953

Jackson, Mississippi, native John W.E. Bowen III was born in 1926. He graduated from Gilbert Academy High School, of New Orleans, Louisiana, as class valedictorian and attended Lincoln University, in Oxford, Pennsylvania, for two years. His college studies were interrupted in June of 1945, when he was drafted into the United States Army. In October of 1946, John received an honorable discharge and resumed his academic studies as a pre-dental student for two years at the University of Southern California.

In 1953 he received an L.L.B. from The Ohio State University School of Law. Thus began his legal career in the Columbus City Attorney's Office where he served as an assistant city attorney, senior assistant city attorney, chief counsel of the office's Civil Division, and first assistant city attorney. After leaving the City Attorney's office, he engaged in private law practice for more than 50 years. He also served as an adjunct professor of law at OSU's College of Law.

John has been active in the United Methodist Church on a national, regional and local basis. His positions include member and vice chairman of the board of trustees, Methodist Union of the Columbus, Ohio District; member of the 1956 Provisional Committee that established Methodist Theological School in Delaware, Ohio; and a member of the board of trustees of the newly established seminary, to name a few.

John served in the Ohio Senate in the 107th and 108th General Assemblies. He was an alternate congressional district delegate from the 15th U.S. Congressional District to the 1956 Republican National Convention in San Francisco, California. Additionally, he was a director of the Federal Home Loan Bank of Cincinnati and served as chairman of its board of directors. He was also a member of the Ohio Board of Regents and the board of directors of the Columbus Area Chamber of Commerce.

John was also a member of the boards of trustees of the Columbus Town Meeting, the Columbus and Franklin County American Red Cross, the Franklin County Mental Health Association, and a former member of the Franklin County Regional Planning Commission.

As one of 100 graduates and one of only two African Americans, John received The Ohio State University Centennial Achievement Award. Ohio Northern University awarded him an Honorary Doctor of Laws degree. He is a life member of Alpha Phi Alpha Fraternity, Inc.

John and his wife, Jeanne Leahr Bowen, are the parents of three daughters and one son. They have four adult grandchildren and one great-grandson.

The Honorable Yvette McGee Brown
Justice
Supreme Court of Ohio

Class of 1985

A series of firsts defines the judicial career of Justice Yvette McGee Brown. She was the first African-American elected to the Franklin County Domestic Relations/Juvenile Court. In January of 2011, she became the first African-American woman to serve as a justice on the Supreme Court of Ohio, and the eighth female justice in the court's history.

McGee Brown was first elected to the Franklin County Court of Common Pleas, Domestic Relations and Juvenile Division in 1992. As lead juvenile court judge, she led the creation of the Family Drug Court and the SMART Program, a truancy and educational neglect intervention program. She served on the Common Pleas Court until 2002, when she retired from the bench to create the Center for Child and Family Advocacy at Nationwide Children's Hospital. The Center is a multi-disciplinary child abuse and family violence program that co-locates prevention, assessment, treatment, research and advocacy services for children and families experiencing abuse. She served as founding president until early 2010, when she became a candidate for lieutenant governor of Ohio. A common theme in McGee Brown's professional and community work is her advocacy for children and families.

McGee Brown graduated from Ohio University in 1982 with a degree in journalism/public relations. She continued her education at The Ohio State University Moritz College of Law, earning a juris doctorate degree in 1985.

An active community and corporate leader, McGee Brown has served on the boards of Ohio University, The Ohio State University Medical Center, the National Council of the OSU Moritz College of Law, M/I Homes, Inc. and Fifth Third Bank of Central Ohio. She is the former chair of the United Way of Central Ohio, The Ohio State University Alumni Association and the YWCA Columbus Board of Directors. In 2008, McGee Brown was inducted into the Ohio Women's Hall of Fame. Among her many honors, she has received the Champion of Children Award, YWCA Woman of Achievement Award and several honors from Ohio University and The Ohio State University.

McGee Brown is married to Tony Brown and they have three children.

The Honorable Kim A. Browne

Judge
Franklin County Court of Common Pleas

Class of 1993

Judge Kim A. Browne was appointed then elected judge of the Franklin County Court of Common Pleas, Domestic Relations and Juvenile Division in 2002. She was twice re-elected, in 2004 and 2010, to full six-year terms. Browne was also twice re-elected as the court's lead juvenile judge and has served as the co-chair of the Franklin County Juvenile Justice Community Planning Initiative or DMC Committee (with City of Columbus Safety Director Mitchell Brown) since March of 2009.

Since January of 2001, Browne has served as an adjunct professor for Ohio Dominican University (ODU). At ODU, she has taught legal environment of business, human resources management and business law for the Master's, Bachelor of Science and Associate degree programs. Browne graduated from The Ohio State University Moritz College of Law in 1993, and from the University of Cincinnati with a baccalaureate degree in economics.

Preceding her appointment to the bench, Browne served as an associate attorney with the law firm of Maguire & Schneider, LLP. Immediately prior, she served as the director of legal operations for the Ohio Bureau of Workers' Compensation, where she also served as the Bureau's director of employee and labor relations and as a state workplace mediator. Earlier in her career, she worked for the Ohio Department of Administrative Services/ Office of Collective Bargaining and for the Ohio Civil Service Employees' Association.

During her tenure on the bench, Browne has created innovative programs to educate and inspire youth to meet and/or exceed their own ambitions, such as the Mini-Moot Court Competition™ for middle and high school-age children and the All Rize College Tour™ for at-risk youth. She oversees the court's Judicial Extern program in collaboration with the OSU Moritz College of Law and Capital University College of Law. Previously, she served on the executive committee of the Ohio Association of Domestic Relations Judges and as a member of the Ohio Supreme Court Rules Advisory Committee.

Married to her husband of 19 years, Steven, the Browne family resides in the Gahanna/New Albany area with their two lovely daughters, Rachel and Regan. MSG Steven Browne serves with the Ohio Army National Guard's 174th Air Defense Artillery.

Quinn Capers IV, M.D., F.A.C.C., F.S.C.A.I.
Associate Dean
Admissions
The Ohio State University, College of Medicine

Class of 1991

Quinn Capers IV is board certified in cardiovascular disease and interventional cardiology, and is the director of peripheral vascular interventions in the Division of Cardiovascular Medicine at The Ohio State University. Recently appointed the associate dean for admissions in the College of Medicine and the first African American to hold the post, he also oversees the admissions process for 4,500 annual applications.

Capers has special expertise in acute coronary syndromes (heart attacks) as well as peripheral vascular disease, and high risk/complex coronary and peripheral vascular interventions. He has published several scientific articles on the topic of pro-inflammatory gene expression in the arterial wall, and has authored several book chapters on the topic of peripheral vascular disease.

A native of Dayton, Ohio, Capers is an alumnus of Howard University and The Ohio State University College of Medicine. He performed his internal medicine residency and fellowships in cardiology research, cardiovascular disease and interventional cardiology at Emory University in Atlanta. Prior to joining The Ohio State University College of Medicine and Medical Center in 2007, he practiced cardiology in Columbus hospitals from 2004 to 2007. Previously, he had a five-year stint in Nashville, Tennessee, in private practice where he was also on the clinical faculty at the city's two medical schools, Vanderbilt University and Meharry Medical College.

He is the recipient of 2009 and 2010 Teaching Excellence awards from OSU medical students and was named one of the Best Doctors in America in 2009 and 2010 on a national survey of physicians. Among Capers' proudest achievements at Ohio State was the pivotal role he played in the successful recruitment of the first African-American cardiology trainees at the OSU College of Medicine since the training program began in the 1950s. In recognition of his efforts and many hours of community service, Capers was awarded the 2010 Ohio State University Distinguished Diversity Enhancement Award as well as the Federal Defense Supply Center Columbus' Carter G. Woodson Award for Community Service.

One of Capers' major goals is to ensure that diversity and health disparities are not forgotten in the current era of health care reform.

Mildred L. Chavous

Retired College Administrator & Community Servant

Mildred L. Chavous served for 32 years in The Ohio State University Graduate School's Office of Educational Administration. At the time of her retirement in 1996, she was the director of graduation services and degrees.

Chavous served on numerous university committees which included the Ohio State Senate Select Committee on Minorities and Women; the search committees for the vice presidents for research, graduates studies and development; the Council on Academic Excellent for Women; the Critical Difference for Women Campaigning Steering Committee; the Ohio State's 300th Commencement Celebration Committee; and the Faculty and Staff Health Care Benefit Committee.

Her community involvement was widespread. She served as a trustee of the Franklin County Board of Retardation and Development Disabilities, Ohio Humanities Council, the Mid-Ohio Health Planning Federation, the Cultural Arts Council Center Advisory Council, Thurber House and Players Theatre.

Chavous has received many awards from the Columbus Coalition of 100 Black Women, the Office of the Mayor of Columbus, Black Women of Courage, Carats, Inc., the Columbus Cancer Clinic and the United Negro College Fund. She likewise received commendations from the Ohio House of Representatives and the Ohio Senate.

She was the first African-American woman president of the Columbus Cancer Clinic, the first African-American woman to chair the United Way Campaign at Ohio State, and the first African-American president of the Pro Musica Sustaining Board.

In addition, Chavous was a founding member of the Twin Rivers Chapter of The Links, Incorporated as well as the society columnist for the *Call & Post* newspaper for more than 15 years.

The Honorable Kimberly Cocroft

Judge
Franklin County Court of Common Pleas

Class of 1995, 1997 and 2000

The Honorable Kimberly Cocroft was appointed judge for the Franklin County Court of Common Pleas on February 24, 2009, by Governor Ted Strickland. Prior to her appointment as judge, she served as deputy legal counsel for Governor Strickland and was responsible for coordinating litigation matters with the chief legal counsels at Ohio's 26 executive agencies, drafting executive orders and directives, and managing legal representation on behalf of Governor Strickland.

Cocroft also served as a law clerk for Justice Alice Robie Resnick at the Supreme Court of Ohio, where she was responsible for drafting opinions that interpret Ohio law. After completing her service at the Ohio Supreme Court, she spent several years in private law practice, specializing in business and employment litigation.

During the November of 2010 election cycle, Cocroft was elected to her first six-year term as a Pleas Court judge by the voters of Franklin County.

Cocroft is a lifelong member of Triedstone Missionary Baptist Church where she has served on its trustee board and Education Ministry, and as a member of several of Triedstone's choirs. She is also an active member of her community through her service as a member of Alpha Kappa Alpha Sorority, Inc., the United Way's Women's Leadership Council, the Alvis House Board of Trustees, and The Harmony Project Choir and Board of Trustees. She is a former board member of the Commission on Continuing Legal Education for the Supreme Court of Ohio, FIRSTLINK and the Gloria S. Friend Christian Academy.

Cocroft is a 1995 and 1997 graduate of The Ohio State University with a Bachelor of Arts degree in psychology and a Master of Arts degree in sport management, respectively. She is also a 2000 graduate of The Moritz College of Law at The Ohio State University.

Dr. Samuel DuBois Cook

President Emeritus
Dillard University

Class of 1950 and 1954

Dr. Samuel DuBois Cook has a distinguished record as a political scientist, scholar, educator, author, teacher, administrator, civil and human rights activist and public servant. A native of Griffin, Georgia, he received a Bachelor of Arts degree from Morehouse College and a Master of Arts and Doctor of Philosophy degrees from The Ohio State University. He taught at Southern University, Atlanta University, the University of Illinois, UCLA and Duke University, where in 1966 he became not only the first black member of the Duke faculty, but also the first black to hold a tenured faculty appointment at a predominantly white Southern college or university. He served 22-and-a-half years as president of historic Dillard University in New Orleans, Louisiana. Upon his retirement in 1997, the board of trustees elected Cook president emeritus of Dillard. Primarily because of his vision, commitment and leadership, Dillard University has the only National Center for Black-Jewish relations in the world.

A member of the Phi Beta Kappa Honor Society, Cook is a Korean War veteran and a former ordained deacon at White Rock Baptist Church in Durham, North Carolina. He holds numerous honorary degrees and is a member of Omega Psi Phi Fraternity, Inc., Pi Sigma Alpha Honor Society, Sigma Pi Phi Fraternity, and numerous professional and civic organizations.

President Jimmy Carter appointed Cook to the prestigious National Council on the Humanities, and President Bill Clinton appointed him to the historic United States Holocaust Memorial Council. He has been chair of the presidents of the United Negro College Fund.

Cook is the author or editor of numerous scholarly publications and was the first black president of the Southern Political Science Association. Previously, he was a member of the editorial boards of the *American Political Science Review* and the *Journal of Politics*.

In 1997 Duke University, where he is a trustee emeritus, established the Samuel DuBois Cook Society, and in 2006, Duke established a postdoctoral fellowship in his honor in its Center for the Study of Race, Ethnicity and Gender in the Social Sciences. The Ohio State University has established the Samuel DuBois Cook Summer Academy and the Samuel DuBois Cook graduate fellowship in political science.

Cook and his wife, Sylvia, have been married more than 50 years and are the parents of Samuel DuBois Cook Jr. and Karen J. Cook. They are members of Ebenezer Baptist Church in Atlanta.

Margot James Copeland
Executive Vice President – Director
Corporate Diversity & Philanthropy
KeyCorp

Class of 1974

Margot James Copeland is executive vice president - director, corporate diversity and philanthropy and an executive council member at KeyCorp, one of the nation's largest bank-based multiline financial services companies. In her role, Copeland also serves as chair of the KeyBank Foundation, guiding the company's strategic philanthropic investment, financial education and workforce development programs that encourage people and communities to achieve economic self-sufficiency.

Copeland holds a Bachelor of Science degree in physics from Hampton University, where she has received the distinguished NAFEO/Alumni Award, and a Master of Arts degree in educational development from The Ohio State University.

Previously, she held positions of increasing responsibility at Xerox Corporation, Polaroid, and Picker International (now Phillips Medical Systems). Prior to joining Key, Copeland served as president and chief executive officer of the Greater Cleveland Roundtable and executive director of Leadership Cleveland. She is a former advisory board member of Firstar NA – Northern Ohio Region (currently US Bank).

She currently serves as trustee of Kent State University, the Thomas White Foundation, the Kenneth Scott Foundation and the Delta Foundation, to name a few. Additionally, Copeland is the national president of The Links, Incorporated, a member of the Executive Leadership Council, and a mentor/protégé program advisor for Morehouse College.

Copeland was a delegate to the White House Conference on America's Future. In addition to her experience leading the Greater Cleveland Roundtable and Leadership Cleveland, Copeland's public service is marked by her appointment to vice chairperson of the Cleveland Bicentennial Commission and subsequently the Cleveland Millennium Commission by former Cleveland Mayor Michael R. White, whose second term Inaugural Committee she chaired.

Her distinguished awards include but are not limited to, one of the 100 Most Influential Blacks in Corporate America from *Savoy* magazine; one of the 100 Most Powerful Women in Cleveland, by *New Cleveland Woman* magazine and the Coalition of 100 Black Women Community Service Award.

A native Virginian, she resides in Cleveland, Ohio, and is the mother of three adult children, Rev. Kimberley S. Copeland, Dr. Garrison E. Copeland and Michael Patterson Taylor Copeland.

Richard Crockett

President & Chief Executive Officer
Capital Transportation, Inc.

Class of 1980

Reared in a household that stressed higher education, hard work and tenacity, the stage was set for success for Richard Crockett at an early age. Currently, the president and chief executive officer of Capital Transportation, Inc., his journey to success was not easy. One of ten children growing up in Mobile, Alabama, Crockett knew that education was his ticket to opportunity. Visiting his sister in Ohio, he had a chance to tour The Ohio State University, from which he would graduate with a bachelor's degree four years later.

Unbeknownst to him, the same department that provided programs to fund his education would be the same one that would sponsor the job fair where he would land his first job in banking with Bank One. Accepted into the Management Training Program, Crockett gained valuable experience in retail, credit and commercial lending. He then served the community as the executive director of a small business lending program through the Ohio Department of Development.

Recognizing a lack of resources in the lending industry for small businesses, Crockett started Capital Resource Group in 1991. An investment banking consulting company, this new venture targeted small businesses to assist in raising the capital needed to grow their companies.

Opportunity presented itself again in 1996, in the form of a small transportation entity. With the help of a handful of employees, Capital Transportation has now become Central Ohio's largest minority-owned transportation services company. Starting with 14 employees, providing school bus transportation, the company has grown to more than 50 employees servicing airports, school districts, military bases, transit authorities and government agencies.

Crockett also spends his time working with several community service organizations. He is a Key Club member with the United Way and co-chairman of the Black Greek Letter Alumni Organization of The Ohio State University. He has sponsored All-Star Basketball Saturday and Easter egg hunts in northeast Columbus for the last 15 years, and often speaks to young African-American males through various programs. Crockett is also a member of Kappa Alpha Psi Fraternity, Inc.

He is most proud of his son, Christopher, a junior at Columbia University who also plays basketball for the college.

Jocelyn Dorsey
Director of Editorials/Public Affairs
WSB-TV, Atlanta, Georgia

The first African-American anchor of a Channel 2 newscast as well as the first African-American news anchor in the Atlanta market, Jocelyn Dorsey has been with WSB-TV for 37 years. She has been director of editorials and public affairs at Channel 2 since 1983. From 1973-83, Jocelyn was an anchor/reporter/producer and assignment editor for WSB-TV's *Channel 2 Action News*. Jocelyn is also executive producer and host of *People 2 People*, a weekly half-hour public affairs program which is broadcast at 6:30 a.m. Sunday mornings on Channel 2.

Jocelyn has won numerous awards for her work with WSB-TV, including seven Southeast Regional EMMYS for Editorial Excellence from the National Academy of Television Arts & Sciences (NATAS). She was the first African American inducted into the SE Region NATAS Silver Circle, for more than 25 years in the field of journalism. She was also the first woman and first African American to receive the Georgia Association of Broadcasters Broadcaster's Citizen of the Year Award, a lifetime achievement award.

Jocelyn has been inducted into the National Association of Black Journalists Region IV-Hall of Fame, and has been named National Media Woman of the Year by the National Association of Media Women. Other civic honors include the YWCA Academy of Women Achievers and the Winnie Mandela Humanitarian Award of Honor, to name a few. She was named Pioneer Black Journalist, the highest award bestowed by the Atlanta Association of Black Journalists.

Her active board affiliations include: Leadership Atlanta, Sisters By Choice, Inc., Piedmont Park Conservancy, and The Real Deal Program. Some of her advisory board affiliations include, The Children's Restoration Network, The National Grandparents Raising Grandchildren's Advisory Board, The National Underground Railroad and the Hands On Atlanta Advisory Council. She is a member of Leadership Atlanta Class of 1989 and the International Women's Forum of Georgia.

Jocelyn is the mother of two sons, the late Teo Gebre-Hiwet and Robert-Fassil Gebre-Hiwet, and the grandmother of four, raising her only granddaughter Zania. She and her family are avid Buckeyes having two generations attending The Ohio State University, where she served as an advisory board member to the School of Journalism.

Ben Espy

Attorney & Lobbyist
Gonzalez Saggio & Harlan, LLP

Class of 1965

Ben Espy earned a Bachelor of Arts degree in political science from The Ohio State University and a juris doctorate degree from Howard University School of Law. Espy has more than 40 years of practice experience in both the public and private sector law. His legal practice has centered on the areas of governmental affairs, litigation, probate and estate planning and school law. He is currently on the staff at Gonzalez Saggio & Harlan, LLP.

Previously, Espy served as the executive assistant attorney general in Ohio, where he had direct supervision over health care fraud, criminal justice initiatives, external government, revenue recovery, special prosecutions, collections enforcement and crime victim services. He was a member of the Columbus City Council for ten years and also served ten years as Ohio State Senator, with the last four years as the minority leader. Espy was the first African-American Ohioan to be the top leader of one of the General Assembly's four legislative caucuses. In his capacity as senator, he served as the ranking minority member on the Finance Committee, Judiciary and State Controlling Board. To his credit, he has received Legislator of the Year awards from the Ohio Association of Local School Superintendents, the Ohio Hunger Task Force and the Franklin County Trial Lawyers Association.

For 25 years, Espy was engaged in the private practice of law with his own firm of Ben Espy Co., LLC in Columbus, Ohio. His firm served as general counsel to the Ohio Association of Elementary School Administrators for 17 years and he was the author of *The Legal Handbook for Ohio School Administrators*, published in 1997. His firm also represented the Ohio Civil Service Employees Association and the Fraternal Order of Police in labor law, civil service matters and federal court litigation. Espy began his career at Allegheny Airlines, where he served as the assistant director of corporate law. He then served in the United States Air Force as a staff judge advocate, where he was voted the Outstanding Lawyer in the Air Defense Command.

Espy is admitted to practice in the state of Ohio; the United States District Court, Northern and Southern Districts of Ohio; the United States Court of Appeals, Sixth Circuit; the Supreme Court of Ohio; the Military Court of Appeals; and the Supreme Court of the United States.

Michael E. Flowers
Vice President & Chief Legal Officer
KBK Enterprises, Inc.

Class of 1979

Michael E. Flowers is vice president and chief legal officer of KBK Enterprises. In addition, Flowers serves as the Columbus city executive for KBK Enterprises with the responsibility to lead and manage the growth of KBK Enterprises in Columbus and surrounding communities. With offices in Columbus, Ohio, Pittsburgh, New Orleans, and Washington, D.C., KBK Enterprises is one of the largest African-American-owned-and-controlled real estate development firms in the United States and currently has real estate development projects underway with a total value in excess of $500 million. The company's real estate development projects include affordable housing and commercial office and retail space.

Prior to joining KBK Enterprises, Flowers was a partner in the Business Law Department of the Ohio-based law firm of Bricker & Eckler, LLP. Active within the American Bar Association, he is currently a member of the editorial board of the *ABA Journal* and is a former chair of the 50,000-member ABA Section of Business Law. Flowers has also engaged in legal reform work in six African countries as a founding member of the ABA Africa Law Council.

Flowers earned a bachelor's degree in business administration from Bucknell University in Lewisburg, Pennsylvania, and a juris doctorate degree from The Moritz College of Law at The Ohio State University; he was named a Distinguished Alumnus of the Law School in 2000. He has completed the Minority Business Executive Program at the Tuck School of Business at Dartmouth and was honored with election to membership in the American Law Institute.

Immediate past chair of the board of trustees for Mount Carmel Health System, Flowers currently serves on the board of trustees for Columbus State Community College and Bucknell University.

Flowers is a deacon at Genessee Avenue Church of Christ. He resides in Worthington with his wife, Jackie, and their son, Darien, and daughter, Andrea.

The Late John L. Francis

Former Columbus City Attorney

Class of 1947 and 1950

Attorney John L. Francis was born in Taylor's Fork, Kentucky. At an early age, his family moved to Wyoming, Ohio. Following high school, Francis moved to Columbus, Ohio, to attend The Ohio State University, where he earned a bachelor's degree in 1947, and a law degree in 1950. He was a member of Omega Psi Phi Fraternity, Inc.

He practiced law for several years before joining the all–black law firm of Brooks, Francis & Bowen, which later became the firm of Bowen, Bell, Francis, White & Saunders, the largest black law firm in Central Ohio.

Francis served as president of the Columbus Branch of the NAACP from 1954 to 1956, and was a member of the NAACP State Board from 1957 to 1964. During his leadership in the NAACP, landmark civil rights cases were litigated in desegregation of housing, elimination of discriminatory vagrancy and suspicious person laws, and establishment of equal employment opportunity laws for transportation workers.

In 1958 Francis became a public defender for the City of Columbus, and in 1964 he was appointed to the Columbus Civil Service Commission. In 1971 he became a judge on the Franklin County Municipal Court, and in 1976 he was appointed as the first black Columbus city attorney.

Francis finished his legal career as an administrative law judge for the Public Utilities Commission of Ohio until his retirement in 1988. After a lingering illness, he passed away on May 31, 1994. He was survived by his wife, Juanita, his sons Dean and Stephen, and his daughters Cynthia and Stephanie.

The Late Juanita J. Francis

Educator

Class of 1948 and 1975

Juanita J. Francis was born in Selma, Alabama, as the oldest of six children. Francis relocated to Youngstown, Ohio, after the death of her mother, and was left to help raise her siblings there. She left Youngstown to attend The Ohio State University, where she earned a Bachelor of Arts degree in mathematics in 1948. She then became one of the first blacks to work in an administrative department at OSU when she took a job as a statistician in the Department of Mathematics upon her graduation. Francis was also a member of the Columbus Black Administrators Association.

Francis later married Attorney John L. Francis, a graduate from The Ohio State University College of Law. She went on to earn a Master of Arts degree in education (guidance and counseling) from The Ohio State University in 1975. Francis was employed for many years as an educator in the Columbus Public Schools, Franklin County Board of MRDD and Cleveland Public Schools systems where she served as a teacher, guidance counselor and principal until her retirement in 1989.

Francis passed away on May 10, 2004, and is survived by her sons, Dean and Stephen, and daughters Cynthia and Stephanie.

Stephen S. Francis

Manager, Diversity Relations
Honda of America Mfg., Inc.

Class of 1984

Stephen Francis is manager of diversity relations within the Administration Division at Honda of America Mfg., Inc. He oversees Honda's cross-functional diversity management initiatives, diversity outreach efforts and supports procurement diversity and staffing activities. Francis is also a member of the Honda of America Foundation Board.

In his role as cross-functional diversity leader for Honda of America, he also helps coordinate Honda diversity efforts across North America for its manufacturing, sales and research and development companies in the areas of minority recruitment, diversity outreach, planning and strategy development.

Francis joined Honda of America in 1995 as an attorney in the Legal Department providing services in the areas of workers' compensation law, benefits, medical and disability programs. He also helped to coordinate legal services for Honda of South Carolina Mfg. Named senior assistant counsel in 1998, his responsibilities were expanded to include leadership roles on projects to develop Honda's Health Insurance Portability and Accountability Act compliance program and the Medically Inactive Transition and Integrated Disability Management programs.

In addition to his Honda responsibilities, Francis is a member of the Columbus Urban League Board, the Columbus Clippers Baseball, Inc. Board of Directors, the Morehouse College Alumni Association, the United Way of Central Ohio Diversity and Inclusion Committee, and the Second Baptist Church Board of Deacons. Francis also is an active volunteer with the American Heart Association.

Francis is a graduate of The Ohio State University College of Law and Morehouse College in Atlanta, Georgia. He and his wife, Carolyn, live in Dublin. They have two sons, Stephen Jr. and John.

The Honorable James E. Green
Judge
Franklin County Municipal Court

Class of 1984

The Honorable James E. Green has served as a judge in the Franklin County Municipal Court for more than 15 years after being appointed by Ohio's Governor in 1995. He has won three contested elections. As a judge, he has presided over more than 300,000 cases, signed in excess of 700 search warrants and performed more than 1,700 weddings. Prior to assuming his judicial role, Green served for five years as an administrator with the Ohio Supreme Court. He also served five years as an assistant county prosecuting attorney.

Green has served as a member of the American Bar Association's Standing Committee on Professionalism, the Ohio Center for Law Related Education, and presently serves as a member of the Ohio State Bar Association's Professionalism and Ethics Committee. He serves and has served as a member of numerous other community, civic and professional organizations.

Placing a high priority on education, he has taught at Columbus State Community College for the past 23 years and regularly speaks at area elementary, middle and high schools. Green founded and supported a scholarship fund at his high school alma mater, is involved in mentoring programs and believes in giving back to his community.

Green was educated in the Akron Public School System in Akron, Ohio. He earned a Bachelor of Arts degree in psychology from the University of Akron in 1980 and a juris doctorate degree from The Ohio State University Moritz College of Law in 1984. He did post doctoral training at the Northwestern University School of Law in 1987.

Prior to attending law school, James worked as a carpenter-cabinetmaker for ten years. During the same time period, he served as a member and officer of the National United Church Ushers Association, where he competed twice for the national championship in the finals of the church ushers' drill team competition.

Green is married and the father of three children.

Archie Griffin

President & Chief Executive Officer
The Ohio State University Alumni Association, Inc.

Class of 1976

Archie Griffin is senior vice president for Alumni Relations and president/chief executive officer of The Ohio State University Alumni Association, Inc. Previously, he was associate director of athletics for Ohio State.

A three-time All-American (1973-1975), Griffin made college football history as the first and only two-time winner of the Heisman Trophy. During his brilliant career, he rushed for an OSU record of 5,589 yards, which helped the Buckeyes capture four Big Ten titles and post an overall record of 40-5-1. He is the only Big Ten player to ever start in four Rose Bowls. In addition to two Heisman Trophies, Griffin has a pair of Silver Footballs, an award presented annually by the *Chicago Tribune* to the Big Ten's MVP. He is one of just three players to win the award twice. Griffin was also a two-time pick as National Player of the Year by both United Press International and the Walter Camp Foundation, winning those awards as a junior and senior. His jersey number "45" was retired September 30, 1999.

Griffin received a degree in industrial relations from OSU in 1976. A fine student, he graduated a quarter early and was chosen as one of the NCAA's top five student athletes as a senior. He received the NCAA's prestigious Top Five Award for combined excellence in athletics, academics and leadership. It is the highest award the NCAA can bestow.

Following graduation, Griffin was a first-round pick of the Cincinnati Bengals. He played eight years of professional football before returning to Columbus and joining the staff at Ohio State.

Ohio State's ambassador of goodwill, Griffin is a member of the Ohio State, Rose Bowl, National Football Foundation, and National High School halls of fame. In 2006, he was listed in NCAA's "100 Most Influential Student-Athletes."

Griffin created the Archie Griffin Scholarship Fund, which benefits Ohio State's Olympic sports programs. He and his wife, Bonita, formed the Archie and Bonita Griffin Foundation Fund that helps develop sports, educational, and travel programs for youth in central Ohio.

Griffin is the spokesperson for the Wendy's High School Heisman Program and is also a member of many charitable organizations, including the Columbus Foundation, Columbus Youth Foundation, and the Columbus Recreation and Parks Commission, to name a few.

He is married to the former Bonita Davis and has three sons, Anthony, Andre, and Adam.

Gene T. Harris, Ph.D.
Superintendent/Chief Executive Officer
Columbus City Schools

Class of 1979

Dr. Gene T. Harris is the 19th superintendent and the chief executive officer of the Columbus City Schools. A Columbus native, she has deep roots in the community and direct experience with public schools as diverse as Ghana and China.

A graduate of Linden-McKinley High School, Harris was admitted to the University of Notre Dame as an upperclassman in the first year the school accepted women. After graduating, she returned to Columbus City Schools to teach English and drama, then moving from the classroom to deputy superintendent in 2000, and superintendent in 2001.

Under the tenure of Harris, Columbus City Schools has focused on improving academic achievement and preparing each student for higher education and work in the global economy. She has accomplished this by cultivating the strong support of the Columbus business community and successfully developing a vision and plan to provide 21st-century learning environments. With the overwhelming support of voters, a 15-year capital improvement plan is underway, which has already resulted in nearly three dozen new and beautifully renovated buildings equipped with the latest technology. The district continues to fulfill levy promises, cutting $76 million from the budget, closing underutilized buildings, renovating older facilities, reducing K-3 average classroom size, providing new school buses, new textbooks and adding critical instruction time back into the day. Harris has targeted parental involvement as key to improving student achievement along with focused professional development for all staff.

Under Harris' leadership, Columbus City Schools is providing innovative programs such as a new international high school, K-8 international studies program, and Science, Technology, Engineering and Match (STEM)-focused schools district-wide.

Harris understands that strong public schools are essential to our city, state and nation's future. As such, she has established a goal of 90% graduation for the Class of 2012.

Harris holds a doctorate from Ohio University, a master's degree from The Ohio State University and a bachelor's degree from Notre Dame. She has twice received the Ingram Award for outstanding leadership as a principal. In 2005, she won the Champion of Children, the Children's Hunger Alliance Educator of the Year, and the Buckingham, Doolittle & Burroughs Stellar Performer awards, among many others.

She is married to Stanley E. Harris, vice president of PNC Bank. Their adult son, Wade Thomas Harris, his wife and son reside in New Jersey.

The Late Isaac D. Harris

Aerodynamic/Flight Test Engineer
1915-1984

Class of 1980

Atlanta native Isaac D. Harris waited 45 years to earn his degree in astronautical/aeronautical engineering. Dropping out of OSU in 1935 in his freshman year to raise a family of five along with his wife, Evelyn, Harris worked 37 years at Wright-Patterson Air Force Base. During that time he hungered to return to the classroom. Retired and at age 60, he went back to the classroom in the winter of 1975. Paying his own way on a retirement income, Harris graduated with a Bachelor of Science degree in 1980. At the time, he was the only African-American graduate in his field. Noting his achievement, the *OSU Quest* wrote a full-page article acknowledging the 65-year-old's triumph.

Harris began his career in 1942 at Wright-Patterson as one of the first five blacks hired as draftsmen by the federal government to fill engineering positions. Because of their race, they were used as file clerks instead of draftsmen. As a result, all five wrote letters to President Truman to force Wright-Patterson to use their qualifications accordingly. President Truman ordered the base commander to use them as engineers; however, little changed and the group fired off another letter. A second order from President Truman threatened to move engineering projects from Wright-Patterson unless the men were used in the capacity for which they were trained. It was then they were given engineering duties.

Harris went on to be promoted many levels and eventually left the base as a flight test aeronautical engineer. While there, he wrote many of the training manuals and conducted pilot trainings. Upon retirement from Wright-Patterson, aircraft companies from across the nation and abroad tried to recruit Harris. He refused, stating he was returning to OSU to earn his degree. Rockwell International indicated that as soon as he graduated they wanted him, and he worked there from 1980-1984.

For seven years after his death, his wife continued to receive calls from companies around the world attempting to recruit Harris. He leaves a legacy of one son who is an aeronautical/structural engineer; two grandsons who are computer and structural engineers, respectively; and one nephew who is a chemical engineer. His grandson, Judge Timothy Horton, is also an OSU graduate from The Moritz College of Law.

Ruth Martin Harriston

Activist & Entrepreneur

Class of 1946

Described as a woman of spirit, determination, courage and strength, Ruth Martin Harriston has been making historical strides for more than 40 years. As a living legend that acted as a forerunner for change, Martin Harriston has created a legacy that will span generations to come. At the age of 81, she continues to look toward the future while appreciating her past.

Marked as a history maker in her own right, Martin Harriston not only affected the move of change from the streets, but challenged the laws of discrimination in employment as well. While pursuing an undergraduate degree in business administration at The Ohio State University, she became one of the first African Americans employed in a clerical position. This change took place when the political science department hired her in her junior year. She graduated in 1946 with a Bachelor of Science degree in business administration.

Advocating for change, Martin Harriston was an iconic figure during the civil rights movement in the city of Columbus. Inspired by Barbee W. Durham, executive director of the Columbus NAACP, Martin Harriston influenced many areas within the organization. She served as secretary of the executive board and chair of the annual membership drive, represented the organization at local churches and assisted in bringing the Little Rock Nine to Columbus. In addition to working for the NAACP, after graduation she became a part of the Ohio Civil Rights Commission, where she became office manager of the central office.

Martin Harriston became the first paralegal to be employed by a major Columbus law firm in 1971. Then at the age of 53, her life took another shift as she founded her own company. She was the first to establish a unique public records search. With her husband, Cardinal, they created Corporate Services of Ohio, Inc.

Though retired, her voice is still being heard. As a writer, Martin Harriston is releasing knowledge and wisdom to this generation through published articles. She also anticipates that one day she will release her own book.

Leonard L. Haynes III, Ph.D.
Director, Institutional Services
Office of Postsecondary Education
U.S. Department of Education

Class of 1975

In April of 2010, Dr. Leonard L. Haynes III was named director of institutional services for the Office of Postsecondary Education, U.S. Department of Education. Previously, he served as executive director for the White House Initiative on Historically Black Colleges and Universities. His distinguished service also includes acting president of Grambling State University, U.S. assistant secretary of postsecondary education and director of academic programs for the United States Information Agency.

A recognized expert on the desegregation of public higher education, especially as it impacts public black colleges, he earned a Bachelor of Arts degree in history from Southern University, a Master of Arts degree in American history from Carnegie-Mellon University, and a Ph.D. in higher education administration from The Ohio State University. Receiving a fellowship from the College of Education, coupled with the opportunity to attend one of the top institutions in the United States, prompted Haynes to enroll at OSU.

Haynes is a member of many notable societies, boards, commissions, civic organizations and professional organizations, including Sigma Pi Phi Fraternity and Omega Psi Phi Fraternity, Inc. In May of 2006, he was recognized by The John Glenn School of Public Service and Management of The Ohio State University as the 16th recipient of the school's annual award for public service. Additionally, he is the recipient of 13 honorary degrees, including one from OSU. Of all the OSU traditions, Haynes most treasures walking the Oval and the football program.

While born in Boston, Massachusetts, Haynes regards himself as a native son of the South. He is married to the former Mary J. Sensley, and they are the proud parents of four children and six grandchildren. An accomplished speaker and presenter, he has served as a commencement speaker and given countless keynotes throughout the United States and abroad. He is a member of Asbury United Methodist Church in Washington, D.C.

Clayton Nathaniel Hicks, O.D.
Owner/Optometrist
Driving Park Vision Center

Class of 1964 and 1970

Dr. Clayton Nathaniel Hicks is the owner of Driving Park Vision Center. He is also a partner and vice president for Outcomes Management Group. Hicks earned a Bachelor of Science degree from The Ohio State University in 1964 and a Doctor of Optometry degree in 1970. While at Ohio State he was vice president of the 1970 class of the OSU College of Optometry. He then served as a clinical instructor for The Ohio State University College of Optometry from 1970 to 1986. Previously, he served as a vision care consultant for the Ohio Department of Jobs and Family Services.

Past president of the National Optometric Association, Hicks is a member of several organizations and affiliations. A few of them include: Alpha Phi Alpha Fraternity, Inc. (president, Columbus chapter, 1981-1983), Alpha Rho Lambda Education Foundation (executive director), the American Public Health Association, the American Optometric Association, the Ohio Optometric Association, Columbus Inner City Lions Club, Epsilon Psi Epsilon Professional Fraternity, the National Coalition of Black Meeting Planners (board of directors), the NAACP and the United Negro College Fund.

Hicks has been a distinguished leader locally and nationally. As a result, he has received numerous honors, awards and recognitions for his service throughout the community. A few of his honors and awards include: Optometrist of the Year (1982), *Who's Who Among Black Americans* (fourth edition), *Who's Who of Emerging Leaders in America* (second edition), *The Who's Who Registry of Global Business Leaders* (1993-94 edition) and the Distinguished Leadership Community Award from the Driving Park Area Commission (1999). The Commission also awarded him the Neighborhood Ambassadorship Award in 2007. Alpha Phi Alpha Fraternity, Inc. awarded Hicks the Theodore Berry Community Service Award in 2007. In 2010 he received the Molina Healthcare of Ohio Community Champions Award.

Ann Wagner Hill, Ph.D.
Educator & Community Leader

Class of 1994

Dr. Ann Wagner Hill is currently retired from the Columbus City and Youngstown Public Schools after serving 40 years as a secondary high school instructor. She has been a visiting professor at The Ohio State University, an adjunct professor at Kenyon College and the assistant admissions director at Sinclair Community College.

Hill received a doctorate degree in global education from The Ohio State University in 1994. Previously, she earned a Bachelor of Science degree from Ohio University and a Master of Education degree from Youngstown State University.

She is the recipient of numerous honors, including the National Endowment for Humanities, Martha Jennings Holden Master Teacher, Kiwanis Community Service, OSU Outstanding Academic, the National Coalition of 100 Black Women and Walnut Ridge Teacher of the Year awards.

Previously, Hill served as the national chairperson for the Black Foot Classic, president of the Carrousels, Inc. and treasurer of the Twin River Chapters of Links, Incorporated. A member of Delta Sigma Theta Sorority, Inc., she currently serves on the advisory board for the Gladys W. and David H. Patton College of Education and Human Services at Ohio University in Athens, Ohio, and is a guest lecturer for the college.

Evidencing her commitment to her students as a teacher and a tour leader, Hill has traveled with her students throughout the country and the world including, Africa, Asia, Europe, and North and South America. She is a motivational speaker for various church groups, women's seminars and professional academic conferences. Likewise, she has made presentations throughout the nation and has several publications to her credit.

In 2003 Hill was inducted into the Negro Hall of Fame. She resides in Columbus with her husband, Tyrone Glenn Hill, and is a member of Triedstone Missionary Baptist Church.

The Honorable Timothy S. Horton
Judge
Franklin County Court of Common Pleas

Class of 1995

In November of 2006, Judge Timothy S. Horton was elected to the Franklin County Court of Common Pleas, General Division. Horton's commitment, knowledge and passion for fairness and justice remain fervent. He is passionate about the law and what it stands for, which is to protect the freedoms and values that we all cherish.

Through the Common Pleas Court, Horton currently serves on the Assigned Counsel, Personnel, Technology and Foreclosure committees. He also serves as the court's liaison for the Franklin County Reentry Task Force. Additionally, he was responsible for implementing the county's first Reentry Docket which reintegrates non-violent offenders into society. Horton is a strong advocate of educating our community and the courts by hosting various civic groups to tour his courtroom with question and answer forums. He has provided students of local schools, from elementary through high school, the opportunity to observe his courtroom.

Outside of the court, Horton is on the board of directors for the Columbus Urban League and Hands On. He was also the recipient of the prestigious *Business First*'s Forty Under 40 Award in 2004. Horton has had various opinions and decisions published in the *Ohio State Bar Association Report*. Additionally, he has been featured in various newspaper articles, *C Magazine* and *Favor Magazine*.

Before taking the bench, Horton practiced at the Columbus law firm of Chester, Willcox & Saxbe, LLP, where he handled complex civil litigation and employment law. He began his career as an Ohio assistant attorney general, where he represented the State of Ohio in federal and state courts that involved employment matters.

In 1995, Horton graduated from The Ohio State University, Moritz College of Law, where he also serves as a guest lecturer and speaker. In 1992, he received an undergraduate degree from Boston University.

Horton, a native of Central Ohio, continues to serve the community through his church, youth soccer associations, and various other boards and associations. He has been married to his wife, Lateea, for 12 years and they have three beautiful and talented children.

Mary Major Jack
President
Major Jack Productions

Class of 1979

Mary Major has proven her versatility and ability to flow in many media environments. Currently, she is president of Major Jack Productions, a television and live-event production company. Mary is also creator and executive producer of *Quiet on the Set*, an hour-long celebrity interview series airing internationally. She has successfully written, produced and directed several television specials that include Turner Broadcast's *Trumpet Awards* and Lifetime Television's *Intimate Portrait: Vanessa Williams*.

Her role as a reporter for *Lifestyles with Robin Leach* includes interviews with notable personalities such as Lena Horne, Halle Berry and Michael Jordan. Similarly, she was a reporter, anchor and producer for *Screen Scene*, a BET celebrity news magazine show. Additionally, she reported for nationally syndicated shows such as *Ebony/Jet Show Case*, and the *World Bodybuilding Championships* on the ESPN network. A recurring role on *The Practice* (ABC) heads the list of acting roles where Mary has been featured. Others include *The Birdcage*, *Kiss the Girls*, and *NYPD Blue* (ABC), to name a few.

Currently, Mary is expanding her television correspondence work as a wellness expert, focusing on lifestyle wellness and expanding Major Jack Productions to producing live events for a myriad of clients including the Urban League. She is also a national motivational speaker, focusing on college-age women and self esteem.

Besides media, Mary recently unveiled her jewelry line called N-er-G, "Healing through Wearing," which is a healing natural stone line that stresses the beauty and healing properties available through the earth. In addition to recent shows at Henri Bendel and Saks Fifth Avenue, her jewelry is available online.

Mary is a 1979 graduate of The Ohio State University with a Bachelor of Arts degree in public relations/communications. There, she was a member of OSU's cheerleading squad from 1976-1979 and represented the university as its homecoming queen in 1978.

The devoted mother of a daughter, Truce, Mary, Kai the dog, and her husband, Michael Jack, president and general manager of the NBC affiliate WNBC, reside in Manhattan.

Keith B. Key
Chief Executive Officer
KBK Enterprises, Inc.

Class of 1989

Born into public housing in Pittsburgh's historic Hill District, Keith B. Key now serves as the chief executive officer of KBK Enterprises, Inc. Key enrolled in The Ohio State University as both a student and football player. Although he didn't make his mark as a football player, Key found his future as a student leader and entrepreneur. He became president of both Omega Psi Phi Fraternity, Inc., and The Ohio State University's college chapter of the NAACP. He served on various committees appointed by the University's president and other leaders, including as a founding student curator of The Ohio State University's Frank Hale Black Cultural Center. He graduated with a Bachelor of Science degree in economics.

Key began his career as a management trainee with Huntington National Bank. Later he joined the consulting firm of PT & Associates. After several years, Key and his colleague, Adam Troy, ventured on their own by forming Omni Management Group, Ltd (OMG). While establishing contracts with various banks including National City Bank and First Merit Bank, OMG secured a contract with the Limited Company and became part of the team that made Easton Town Center, a retail success on 1,200 acres, a reality. Key soon established KBK Enterprises in an effort to take his commercial and housing developmental skills nationwide.

Today, KBK Enterprises is active in various cities in Ohio and throughout the nation including Pittsburgh, Washington, D.C., New York, Chicago and New Orleans. In addition to real estate development, KBK has engaged in various business ventures to maximize other entrepreneurial endeavors. With more than $500 million in current activities under contract, Key has been involved with more than a billion dollars worth of projects in his career.

As a former public housing resident with a stuttering condition, raised in a single parent home, Key has become one of America's most unique success stories. He is married to Donica D. Key, and they have three children, Danielle, Darienne, and K. Brandon.

The Late Robert Henry Lawrence Jr.

Astronaut
United States Air Force

Class of 1965

Robert Henry Lawrence Jr. was a United States Air Force officer and the first African American selected for astronaut training. He graduated high school at the age of 16 in the top ten percent of his class. He later graduated with a bachelor's degree from Bradley University and went on to serve in the Air Force. At the age of 21, he was designated as a U.S. Air Force (USAF) pilot after completing flight training at Malden Air Force Base. By the time he was 25, Lawrence had completed an Air Force assignment as an instructor pilot in the T-33 training aircraft for the German Air Force. His legacy at The Ohio State University began in 1965 when he earned a Ph.D. in physical chemistry.

A senior USAF pilot, he accumulated well over 2,500 flight hours—2,000 of which were in jets. Lawrence flew many tests in the Lockheed F-104 Starfighter to investigate the gliding flight of various unpowered spacecraft returning to Earth from orbit, such as the North American X-15 rocket-plane. NASA cited Lawrence for accomplishments and flight maneuver data that "contributed greatly to the development of the Space Shuttle."

In June of 1967, Lawrence successfully completed the Air Force Flight Test Pilot Training School at Edwards Air Force Base in California. That same month he was selected by the USAF as an astronaut in the Air Force's Manned Orbital Laboratory (MOL) program, thus becoming the first black astronaut.

Lawrence was killed on December 8, 1967, in the crash of an F-104 Starfighter at Edwards Air Force Base, California. Had Lawrence lived, he likely would have been among the MOL astronauts who transferred to NASA after the program's cancellation, all of whom flew on the Space Shuttle.

During his brief career, Lawrence earned the Air Force Commendation Medal, the Outstanding Unit Citation, and was posthumously awarded the Purple Heart medal. After many years of relative obscurity, on December 8, 1997, his name was inscribed on the Space Mirror Memorial at the Kennedy Space Center in Florida.

Dr. Valerie B. Lee
Vice Provost & Chief Diversity Officer
Office of Diversity and Inclusion
The Ohio State University

Class of 1976

Dr. Valerie B. Lee is vice provost for the Office of Diversity and Inclusion (ODI) and chief diversity officer at The Ohio State University (OSU). She is also the first woman and African American to have chaired the OSU English Department. Prior to chairing English, she chaired the Department of Women's Studies. An interdisciplinary scholar, Lee also holds courtesy appointments in African-American and African Studies, Folklore Studies, Comparative Studies, and Interdisciplinary Law and Policy Studies.

Lee has published dozens of articles and authored several books, including *Granny Midwives and Black Women Writers: Double-Dutched Readings* and *The Prentice-Hall Anthology of African American Women's Literature*. She teaches classes in law and narrative and African-American literature, culture and theory.

Her awards include the OSU Alumni Distinguished Teacher Award, the OSU Distinguished Service Award, and the 2005 YWCA Woman of Achievement Award. For many years, she chaired the University Diversity Council and was the 2007 national president of the Association of Departments of English.

Lee is married to James C. Lee, Esquire, and they are the parents of Erica, Jessica, Adam, and Andrew.

Samella Sanders Lewis

Artist and Art Historian

Class of 1948 and 1951

Samella Sanders Lewis is considered a pioneer in the African-American art world. A native of New Orleans, Louisiana, she used art to express her life and surroundings. Drawing from the age of four, Lewis' career of more than 50 years includes painter, graphic artist, sculptor, author, entrepreneur and educator.

As an art student at Dillard University, Lewis studied under the renowned sculptor, Elizabeth Catlett. She transferred to Hampton Institute where she graduated in 1945, earning a degree in art history. After teaching at Hampton for one year, she entered The Ohio State University, where she obtained a Master of Arts degree in 1948. In 1951 she earned a Ph.D., becoming Ohio State's first dual-doctorate major in fine arts and art history.

Lewis held several teaching positions at colleges throughout the United States, including Morgan State University, Florida A&M University, the State University of New York College at Plattsburgh and California State University at Long Beach. From 1969 to 1984, Lewis was an art history professor at Scripps College in Claremont, California, and became Scripps' first tenured African-American professor. In her honor, the college has established the Samella Lewis Contemporary Art Collection.

Another first in her life came when she founded Contemporary Crafts, the first African-American-owned art publishing house. Lewis and East High School graduate and artist Bernie Casey founded the Contemporary Crafts Gallery, which served as a showcase for African-American artists. In addition, she has written five books and catalogued for or curated nine shows. Lewis wrote the first textbook on African-American art history, *Art: African-American*.

Lewis was the recipient of a Fulbright Foundation fellowship and numerous awards and honors. Through the years she has served as founder of the Museum of African American Art in Los Angeles, a project director for the National Endowment for the Arts and editor of the *International Review of African-American Art*, which she established in 1976.

Married to Paul Lewis, she has two sons, Alan and Claude, and two grandchildren.

The Late Colonel George A. Martin, M.D.
Deputy Commander
United States Air Force

Class of 1980 and 1989

Colonel George A. Martin was born in Munich Germany. He graduated from The Ohio State University with a Bachelor of Science degree in microbiology. Martin entered the United States Air Force in May of 1981 as a missile launch officer at Whiteman Air Force Base (AFB). In 1984 he earned a Master of Science degree in industrial hygiene and safety from Central Missouri State University.

After completing his initial tour of duty, he received a Doctorate of Medicine degree from The Ohio State University, College of Medicine. He re-entered the active duty Air Force as a medical doctor in July of 1990 and attended John Hopkins residency training in emergency medicine.

In June of 1995, Martin was assigned to the medical office of NASA, Kennedy Space Center. In August of 1998, he was the commander, Aerospace Medicine Flight 36 MDG, Anderson AFB. From there he served at Hanscom AFB, Massachusetts; Kadena AFB, Japan; Camp Navaro, Florida; MacDill AFB, Florida; and Tallil AFB in Iraq before returning to the 36th Medical Group at Anderson AFB in Guam as the deputy commander.

Martin served two missions in Bagdad, Iraq, as a general surgeon in one of the largest hospitals in Bagdad. His outstanding clinical direction led to the successful evacuation of more than 3,500 ill or injured patients in direct support of Operations Iraqi Freedom and Enduring Freedom. Martin's first-hand knowledge of combat medicine enabled him to effectively manage the many patient complexities and air evacuation issues in the most intensive month of fighting in Iraq.

Martin aspired to be an astronaut and go to Mars. He had been to the Haughton-Mars Project three times, in 1998, in 2000 and 2002. However, he met an untimely death in 2008 when the B-52 bomber on which he was a crew member crashed during a fly-by flight in celebration of Guam's Liberation Day.

Martin is survived by wife Ursula Te'o Martin, daughter Gemini Martin and son Guahan Te'o Martin.

The Honorable Stephen Louis McIntosh

Judge
Franklin County Court of Common Pleas

Class of 1983

Judge Stephen L. McIntosh was born in Columbia, South Carolina. He is married to Sara A. McIntosh, M.D. and they have three children. He proudly serves as a deacon at Second Baptist Church. McIntosh received an undergraduate degree from South Carolina State University and a law degree from The Ohio State University Moritz College of Law. He received the Judge Joseph Harter Trial Advocacy Award.

Prior to serving on the bench, he worked as deputy director of the Uniform Commercial Code Division of Ohio Secretary of State Sherrod Brown's office, an associate at the law firm of Crabbe, Brown, Jones, Potts and Schmidt, (now Crabbe Brown and James) and as chief prosecutor for Columbus City Attorney Janet E. Jackson and Richard C. Pfeiffer.

McIntosh has always been active in the legal profession and community. In 2010 he became president of the Board of Governors of the Columbus Bar Association. He is a member of the John Mercer Langston Bar Association and the Ohio State Bar Association, where he serves on the Council of Delegates and the Legal Ethics and Professional Conduct Committee. McIntosh currently serves on the Supreme Court Advisory Committee on Dispute Resolution, the Supreme Court Advisory Committee on Interpreter Services, the Ohio Lawyer Assistance Fund Board and the Continuing Legal Education Commission. In the community, McIntosh is a board member with Alvis House and the Gahanna YMCA. Previously, he served as the legal advisor for the Marion Franklin High School Mock Trial team for 15 years. He has authored numerous articles for the Columbus Bar Association including "Straight Talk About the Law, the Role of the Public Prosecutors," and the role of "Plea Bargaining," in criminal cases.

In 2001 McIntosh was appointed special prosecutor for the City of Cincinnati in the case of *City of Cincinnati v. Stephen Roach*. This case involved the shooting of a young African-American male, which sparked days of rioting within the city of Cincinnati.

McIntosh's aspiration is to make a difference in the profession and the community. His faith in God and family support has been significant throughout his life.

Charles McMurray Jr.

Special Assistant to the President & Chief Executive Officer
The Ohio State University Alumni Association, Inc.

Class of 1950

After serving in the Navy from 1943 to 1946, Charles McMurray Jr. came to Ohio State in 1947. He graduated in 1950 with a Bachelor of Science degree in social administration. Since 1991 he has served as the special assistant to the president and chief executive officer of The Ohio State University Association Alumni Association, Inc. In this position, McMurray strengthens the association's role in government and community relations, and is involved in alumni programming for minorities, the Black Alumni Society and minority student recruitment.

Previously, he spent 23 years (1968-1991) at Ohio Bell Telephone Company in a variety of management roles such as community relations manager; manager, centralized repair bureau; and commercial manager for urban affairs. McMurray also spent 16 years as a probation officer and intake supervisor with the Franklin County Court of Domestic Relations Juvenile Division.

For several years, McMurray was a booking agent for Jesse Owens. Traveling with Owens throughout the United States, he arranged speaking engagements in the Midwest, sometimes as many as two to three times per day. The two remained friends and confidantes until Owens' death in 1980.

To his credit, McMurray's community involvement has been extensive. He served on the boards of directors for numerous organizations, including the American Red Cross, the Columbus Urban League, Capitol Square Commission (mayoral appointment) and the Boys Club of Columbus, to name a few. He likewise served on the board of governors for WOSU radio and television stations, was a member of The Ohio State University Athletic Council, and a board trustee for the Martin Luther King Performing and Cultural Arts Complex.

A member of Kappa Alpha Psi Fraternity, Inc., McMurray received the OSU Distinguished Service Award, the OSU William Henry Watson Award and the Boys Club of America Bronze Keystone Award. The Ohio House of Representatives twice recognized him for receiving these awards.

McMurray is married to Colleen and is the father of three children, Kim, Mark and Trent.

Marquis D. Miller

Vice President, Field Operations
National Minority Supplier Development Council

Class of 1981

Marquis D. Miller was recently named vice president of field operations for the National Minority Supplier Development Council, Inc.® (NMSDC®), one of the nation's leading corporate membership organizations, effective Monday, January 3, 2011. Miller works with the NMSDC president to maximize organizational performance among the Council's 37 affiliates. He also works collaboratively with the affiliates to help align resources, plans, strategies and actions with NMSDC's mission, and enhance the services provided to NMSDC-certified Asian, Black, Hispanic and Native American businesses.

Previously, Miller was head of The Business Mosaic, a consulting practice focused on organizational management in the nonprofit, consumer/retail and business services sectors. Prior to that, Miller was vice president of business development for SBLI USA Mutual Life Insurance and S. USA Life, a wholly-owned subsidiary of SBLI USA Mutual Life Insurance Company in Chicago's Loop. He has also served as interim vice president of institutional advancement at Chicago State University (CSU), executive director of the CSU Foundation, vice president of external affairs for the Chicago Urban League and vice president of the Corporate Scholars Program of the United Negro College Fund (UNCF). Prior to that role, Miller was vice president of field operations for the UNCF's Midwest office in Chicago.

Miller earned a bachelor's degree in social and behavioral sciences from The Ohio State University in 1981, where he lettered for four years on the men's basketball team. He is a member of the Varsity "O" Men's Alumni Association.

He serves on the board of trustees for the Museum of Contemporary Art and is a board member of GRANDfamilies Program of Chicago.

Miller resides in Chicago with his wife Pamela.

Curtis J. Moody
President & Chief Executive Officer
Moody•Nolan, Inc.

Class of 1973

For more than 35 years, Curtis J. Moody has been designing a successful career in architecture. As a registered architect in more than 30 states, as well as being NCARB-certified and a LEED AP, he has built the largest African-American-owned-and-operated architectural and engineering firm in the nation. The Columbus, Ohio, headquartered firm, entering into its 29th year, has a staff of more than 170 professionals and regional offices in Covington/Cincinnati, Cleveland, Indianapolis, Nashville, Kansas City, Missouri, and Washington, D.C. In the fall of 2010, the firm opened an eighth office in Chicago.

Upon his 1973 graduation with a Bachelor of Science degree in architecture from The Ohio State University, Moody apprenticed for several Columbus-area design firms. He started his own firm, Moody and Associates, in 1982. Designing a new building, The New Life Apostolic Church, was the first project for this young firm. Quickly, Moody's success evolved, and just two years later he joined forces with engineer Howard Nolan to form Moody/Nolan Ltd., Inc. Today, Moody•Nolan offers services in architecture, civil engineering, interior design and planning. The firm has experienced steady growth across a variety of project types including: sports and recreation, health care, education, housing, aviation and major public works.

Moody•Nolan's innovative design and extraordinary value has been recognized over the years with more than 160 design citations and awards, including the 2007 Gold Medal from The American Institute of Architects (AIA), Ohio Chapter, the 2006 Gold Medal Firm of the Year Award from AIA, Ohio Chapter, as well as the inaugural 2000-2001 Firm of the Year Award given by the National Organization of Minority Architects (NOMA).

Additionally, Moody has been personally acknowledged by his peers and clients. In 1997, he was honored with a Fellowship in The American Institute of Architects, the highest recognition bestowed by that organization and the only architect in the state of Ohio to receive this prestigious honor. He continues his dedication to the advancement of the architecture profession by remaining active in several associations in the architecture industry and the community. He was recognized in 1995 with the Entrepreneur of the Year Award in the Service Category. In 1992, he was awarded the national Whitney M. Young, Jr. Award given to one outstanding minority architect by The American Institute of Architects, Washington, D.C. More recently, Moody was appointed to serve as a peer reviewer for the Architect/Engineer Selection Panel for the General Services Administration Design Excellence Program.

Moody is a life-long resident of Columbus, Ohio. He and his wife, Elaine, have three sons. Hobbies for the Moody family include boating, fishing and the beach.

Frederick L. Ransier
Partner
Vorys, Sater, Seymour and Pease, LLP

Class of 1974

Fred Ransier is a partner in the Vorys Columbus office and a member of the bankruptcy and government affairs and lobbying groups. Fred received his juris doctorate degree from The Ohio State University Michael E. Moritz College of Law in 1974 and his Bachelor of Arts degree from Central State University in 1971.

He began his legal career as an Ohio assistant attorney general in the Criminal Activities Section, from 1974 to 1976. In 1976, in Columbus, along with his wife and law school classmate, Kathleen H. Ransier (Kathy), he opened Ransier & Ransier, where he and Kathy practiced continually until 2001. In 2001 the Ransiers joined as partners in the Columbus office of Vorys, Sater, Seymour and Pease, LLP.

Fred has served as a bankruptcy trustee for the Southern District of Ohio since 1988 and represents clients in commercial and real estate matters. He was admitted to practice by The Supreme Court of Ohio in 1974, and is admitted to practice before the United States District Court for the Southern District of Ohio, the United States District Court for the Northern District of Ohio, and the United States Court of Appeals for the Sixth Circuit. He is currently an active member of the National Association of Bankruptcy Trustees, the National Bar Association, the American Bankruptcy Institute, the Ohio Bar Association and the Columbus Bar Association.

Prior community service includes serving on numerous boards including the Columbus College of Art and Design, the Franklin Park Conservatory Joint Recreation District, Experience Columbus, and Central State University, to name a few. In addition, he was a member of The Ohio State University Alumni Association, Inc. Alumni Advisory Committee and the Municipal Civil Service Commission for the City of Columbus. Currently, he serves on The Ohio State University and Columbus Metropolitan Housing Oversight Committee and the Near East Side Advisory Committee. He has been a fellow of the Columbus Bar Foundation since 1992.

In 2010 *Columbus CEO* named Fred one of the Top Lawyers in Columbus. He has received The Ohio State University College of Law Alumni Community Service Award and the Central State University Alumni Association Alumnus of the Year Award. In addition, he was awarded a Presidential Citation from the National Association for Equal Opportunity in Higher Education.

Kathleen H. Ransier
Partner
Vorys, Sater, Seymour and Pease, LLP

Class of 1974

Kathleen Ransier joined Vorys, Sater, Seymour and Pease in 2001. Prior to joining Vorys, Kathy and her husband, Fred Ransier, were managing partners of their own private law practice, Ransier & Ransier, which they opened in 1976. Before opening her own practice, Kathy was a staff attorney at the Ohio Department of Commerce, Division of Securities. A 1969 graduate of Western College, she is also a 1974 graduate of The Ohio State University Moritz College of Law.

Kathy has been appointed to numerous positions by local, state and educational bodies, including commissioner, Court of Claims of Ohio; member, Committee on Court Technology, Ohio Supreme Court; special counsel, Ohio Attorney General; special counsel, Franklin County Common Pleas Court, Probate Division; and the Supreme Court of Ohio Commission on Professionalism.

She has been tapped to serve on several boards of directors and trustees, including a public company, educational institutions, civic organizations and nonprofits. Currently, she serves as a member of the board of trustees or directors of the following: Huntington Bancshares Incorporated, The Ohio State University Alumni Association, Inc., Capital University Advisory Board, the Columbus Arts Endowment, the Columbus Regional Airport Authority (chair), and the Capital Club, to name a few.

A member of the American Bar Association, she also holds membership with the Ohio State Bar Association, the Columbus Bar Association and the Columbus Bar Foundation. She served as a trustee of the Columbus Bar Foundation from 1992 to 1996 and has been a fellow since 1992.

Her community involvement and professional service has resulted in numerous honors, including the Constance Baker Motley Award, NAACP Legal Defense and Education Fund, Inc.; the Black Business Award, The Council of Black Students in Administration, The Ohio State University; Community Service Award, The Ohio State University, Moritz College of Law; YWCA Women of Achievement Award; and the Community Service Award, Western College for Women, to name a few.

Kathy has presented numerous continuing legal education seminars in real estate, women in the law and marketing. She has also lectured at The Ohio State University College of Business and The Moritz College of Law and has presented seminars sponsored by the Columbus Minority Contractor/Business Assistance Program and the U.S. Small Business Administration.

The Honorable Guy L. Reece II

Judge
Franklin County Court of Common Pleas

Class of 1981

Judge Guy L. Reece II, was appointed to the Franklin County Common Pleas Court in 2003, and re-elected in 2006. He previously served as a Municipal Court judge (1990-1991). He resigned from the bench in 1995, to accompany his wife on her corporate career opportunity in Indonesia. During his three years in Indonesia, he was a legal advisor with an Indonesian law firm and a consultant to several businesses. Prior to his appointment to the court in 2003, he served as the director of the Franklin County Board of Elections.

Reece received an undergraduate degree from the University of Nebraska-Omaha in 1972. He is a 1981 graduate of The Ohio State University Moritz College of Law. He started his legal career with the Columbus City Attorney's Office and from there was first elected to judicial office.

Reece is a Vietnam War Veteran and a retired Colonel of the U.S. Army, where he earned numerous awards including the Bronze Star. He is also a graduate of The United States Army War College.

A member of the John Mercer Langston Bar Association, Reece is also a member of the Columbus Bar Association, the Ohio State Bar Association, the American Bar Association and the National Bar Association. He is vice president of the Ohio Common Pleas Judges Association and is on the executive board of the State National Conference of Trial Court Judges. He is a recipient of The Ohio State University's Minority Alumni Award and its Affirmative Action Award.

Reece is actively involved in many volunteer and charitable activities in his community. He is the past chairman of the Metropolitan YMCA Board of Central Ohio and is a member of the boards of trustees of Ohio Dominican University, Maryhaven, Directions for Youth and Families and the Ohio Veterans Hall of Fame Foundation. He is the chair of the Capital City District, Simon Kenton Council of the Boy Scouts of America. He also currently serves as a deacon at Second Baptist Church in Columbus.

Reece enjoys cooking, reading, golf and traveling. He and his wife, Shirley, have three children and three grandchildren. The couple resides in Blacklick, Ohio.

Robert C. Reed
Founder & Chief Executive Officer
RCR Technology Corporation

Class of 1982

With honesty and integrity, Robert C. Reed has built a solid professional career in Indianapolis as a leader in information technology (IT). He is founder and chief executive officer of the RCR Technology Corporation, an innovative IT consulting firm that has prospered as a leader among data management solutions and technology-driven, middle-market companies. The late Mayor Harold Washington of Chicago, a strong advocate of minority businesses, inspired Robert to venture out on his own.

RCR's clients have included the Indiana Family and Social Services Administration, EDS, Hewlett-Packard and IBM; the company has offices in Indianapolis, Cleveland and Atlanta. Recently, the *Indianapolis Business Journal* ranked the company eighth on its list of the largest Indianapolis area minority-owned businesses.

RCR Technology is a sponsor of the Indiana Black Expo Technology Center and the Kids Voices Charity. The company also received the Governor's Technology Company of the Year Award. Robert is affiliated with the Indiana Minority Supplier Development Council, and is a member of 100 Black Men of Indianapolis, Inc. He serves on the board of directors for the Madame Walker Theatre Center.

A native of Cleveland, Ohio, Robert completed his undergraduate studies in 1982 at The Ohio State University, where he worked toward a bachelor's degree in computer science. Robert and his wife, Sharon Robinson Reed, reside in Fishers, Indiana, with their two daughters, Lindsey and Lauren.

Rev. Dr. Barbara A. Reynolds

Journalist & Author

Class of 1967

The Reverend Dr. Barbara A. Reynolds is an award-winning journalist and author and has appeared on major television shows and networks, such as *The Oprah Winfrey Show*, *Politically Incorrect*, C-SPAN and CNN. For a decade she was heard on XM satellite radio and WOL-AM on her own signature show called, *Reynolds Rap*. She is also president of WCAN (Women's Christian Action Network) a new multimedia television channel that will be launched in 2011.

Reynolds has more than 30 years of experience as a journalist / writer with some of the major media institutions, such as *Ebony*, *Essence* and the *Chicago Tribune*. In addition, she was a founding start-up editor with *USA Today*, where she was an editorial board member and columnist for more than 13 years. Today, she is a religion columnist for the National Newspaper Publishers Association, which reports a readership of ten million.

Born in Columbus, Ohio, Reynolds received a Bachelor of Arts degree in journalism from The Ohio State University, a master's degree from Howard University School of Divinity, and a doctorate degree in ministry from the United Theological Seminary in Dayton, Ohio. She has been awarded honorary doctorates in humane letters from Shenandoah University and The Ohio State University.

Bishop Alfred A. Owens Jr. ordained Reynolds an elder at the Greater Mt. Calvary Holy Church in 1995. She has preached in many churches and for many denominations across the United States. Her books include: *Jesse Jackson: America's David*, an unauthorized biography, *And Still We Rise: Interviews with 50 African-American Role Models*; and *No I Won't Shut Up! 30 Years of Telling It Like It Is*, to name a few.

Reynolds' many honors include the Martin Luther King Jr. Drum Major for Justice Award, the 1999 Journalist of the Year Award from the National Association of Black Journalists and the Outstanding Life Time Achievement Award from the Columbia University (Missouri) School of Journalism. In 1976 she became one of the first African-American women to receive a Nieman Fellowship at Harvard University where she studied constitutional law.

She lives in Prince George's County with her son, John Eric Reynolds.

Carl D. Smallwood
Partner
Vorys, Sater, Seymour and Pease, LLP

Class of 1977 and 1980

Carl D. Smallwood is a partner in the Columbus office of Vorys, Sater, Seymour and Pease law firm. After earning a Bachelor of Science degree in business administration and international business at The Ohio State University in 1977 and a juris doctorate degree from the university's Moritz College of Law in 1980, Smallwood joined Vorys in 1980, becoming a partner in 1987.

Smallwood's active and distinguished service resulted in his election, in 2000, as the first African-American president of the 4,800-member Columbus Bar Association. On a national level, he currently serves as an officer on the Executive Council of the National Conference of Bar Presidents of the American Bar Association, and served in the House of Delegates from 2002-2006. He also serves as president of the Law and Leadership Institute, LLC, a statewide diversity pipeline program in Ohio for promising high school students from underserved communities interested in the legal profession.

A loyal and passionate Ohio State alumnus, Smallwood continues his active involvement with his alma mater, where he has served as president of the Law Alumni Society, the Black Law Alumni Society and the Black Law Students Association. A member of The Moritz College of Law National Council from 1998 to 2008, he previously served as an adjunct professor in trial advocacy. Additionally, as a result of having lettered in varsity soccer in 1974 and 1976, he is a member of the Varsity "O" Club.

The Ohio State University Alumni Association recognized him with the Josephine Failer Award for service to students in 1994 and the Heinlen Award for university advocacy in 2001. At the March 2010 Winter Commencement, he received The Ohio State University's Distinguished Service Medal.

He is the second Smallwood to serve OSU. His late father, Dr. Osborn T. Smallwood, served as director and vice president for international affairs at OSU in the 1970s.

Smallwood serves on the board of Gladden Community House, a settlement house offering neighborhood-based social services to individuals, families and groups on the near west side of Columbus. He is happily married to Connie Harris Smallwood (OSU '78, '81), and they have two children.

Lewis R. Smoot Jr.
Senior Vice President
Smoot Construction

Class of 1994

Since joining the firm in 1980, Lewis Smoot Jr. has held positions of increasing responsibility including laborer, estimator, project manager and administrative manager. In July of 2010, he was promoted to senior vice president and currently provides direction and leadership for several corporate initiatives, including business strategy and administration, information technology and computer operations, safety, budgeting and capital expenditures management, general business policies and procedures, community and public relations, and EEO. He was appointed to The Smoot Corporation board of directors in 2005. Lewis also serves as a member of the Corporate Executive Committee and represents the third generation of leadership for the firm.

His specific responsibilities include: providing direction and advice relative to corporate administrative programs and procedures including the firm's financial resources and position (including bonding capacity), risk management and employee benefits programs. He also oversees the corporate safety program to ensure all company and regulatory guidelines and standards are maintained. He has championed the development of a dynamic work environment by exemplifying and celebrating fairness, creativity and integrity, and promoted a healthy spirit of competition to provide maximum benefit to the shareholders, employees, clients and the community.

Lewis represents the corporation to various external organizations on such matters as the firm's general operational policies and procedures, and proactive EEO and public relations programs. He also facilitates and supports the firm's business development and marketing efforts through increasing prospective clients' awareness regarding the company's character, policies, skills, resources and capabilities and achievements.

Lewis' previous project experience includes the Fleet Management and Maintenance Facility for the City of Columbus. This 150,000-square-foot facility consolidates operations for maintaining motorized equipment for various City of Columbus departments and divisions. Additionally, he has managed the Thompson Library Renovation at The Ohio State University. This complex project involved extensive demolition and new construction for the restoration, renovation and expansion of this historic landmark. His other significant projects include the Rosewind HOPE VI, Columbus Metropolitan Housing Authority construction and public housing development for multi-family and single family units as well as the Medical Logistics Facility for The Ohio State University.

Lewis attended The Ohio State University and earned a Bachelor of Science degree in industrial technologies in 1994.

Jesse J. Tyson

Global Aviation Director
ExxonMobil

Class of 1976

Today, Jesse Tyson leads the global aviation business for ExxonMobil based in Brussels, Belgium, with primary responsibility for strategic development of sustainable solutions, customer needs, return requirements and operational issues within 50 countries and with more than 1,000 clients. This includes airlines, militaries, joint ventures, airport authorities and industry associations.

Prior to this assignment, Tyson led ExxonMobil Americas South fuels marketing efforts as president and marketing director of ExxonMobil Inter-America. As chief of this group, his responsibilities included the retail fuels business across controlled and free markets. He represented ExxonMobil with the Council of the Americas, the Departments of Commerce, State and Energy, the Office of the United States Trade Representative and host governments to ensure balanced implementation of regulations.

Earlier Tyson served as the global customer service leader responsible for distribution, road transportation and order-to-cash management. In addition, he has many years of experience on efficiency, risk management and safety projects. He is considered a marketing expert having served in many marketing positions within Exxon's United States and international business.

Tyson holds a Bachelor of Science degree in economics and business from Lane College and an MBA from The Ohio State University. He attended the Brookings Institute and The International Management Development School in Switzerland.

He is a past board member of Florida A&M University; The Ensemble Theatre and Children's Museum in Houston; the Dean's Executive Advisory Board at Florida International University; and the board of directors of the Foundation for Management Education in Central America. Currently, he serves on the advisory board of the Fisher College of Business at The Ohio State University. Tyson was named one of the Twelve Good Men by the Ronald McDonald House and is a recipient of numerous awards and honorable mentions including the 2009 *Black Enterprise* Most Influential Black Executive. Often sought as an inspirational speaker to youth across the country, he is also a member of Alpha Phi Alpha Fraternity Inc., Sigma Pi Phi Fraternity and The Executive Leadership Council.

Jesse and his wife, Cheryl, live in Brussels and are the proud parents of three adult daughters and one grandson.

James N. Upton, Ph.D.

Faculty Emeritus
African American and African Studies
The Ohio State University

Class of 1971, 1974 and 1976

James N. Upton, Ph.D., is an emeritus faculty in the African American and African Studies Department (AAAS) at The Ohio State University. He teaches graduate and undergraduate courses about African-American social and political philosophy, social science research methodology, and social movements.

Upton has presented numerous papers at national and international conferences and Fulbright colloquia in England, Northern Ireland, France, and Canada. His recent published works include the reexamination of race as a nationality concept in American society, and his current research is a comparison of social movements and political protest in the United States and England.

On a national level, Upton testified before the Oklahoma House of Representatives' Special Committee on Affirmative Action in Higher Education and the U.S. Commission on Civil Rights regarding affirmative action and civil rights issues in higher education. He participated as a faculty advisor in the OSU Honors study abroad tour of England in 2005.

Upton earned Bachelor of Arts, Master of Arts, and Doctorate of Philosophy degrees in political science from The Ohio State University. He was the recipient of a Rockefeller Foundation Research Fellowship and received a 2005 Alumni Award for Distinguished Teaching from The Ohio State University.

Lewis Walker, Ph.D.
Emeritus Chair & Professor of Sociology
Western Michigan University

Class of 1961 and 1964

Dr. Lewis Walker is emeritus chair and professor of sociology at Western Michigan University. His specialties include race/ethnic relations, criminology and social psychology. He has been a professor to more than 22,000 undergraduate and graduate students, and spent a significant part of the last 45 years teaching, researching, conducting demonstration projects, and serving as a consultant to various public and private organizations.

Walker is the author and/or co-author of seven books, numerous scholarly papers and published articles. Among his most recent co-authored books are two with Dr. Benjamin C. Wilson, namely: *African Americans in Michigan* and *Black Eden: The Idlewild Community*. *Black Eden* was listed as One of Twenty Must Read Books in Michigan. He recently completed a six-volume DVD/video project involving a socio-historical view of South Africa.

A native of Selma, Alabama, Walker is the recipient of numerous awards. In 2000 Western Michigan University renamed its race institute the Lewis Walker Institute for the Study of Race and Ethnic Relations for his outstanding work in the field. The City of Kalamazoo, Michigan, created the Dr. Lewis Walker Community Youth Justice Service Award in 2001 to recognize his numerous contributions to social justice. The award is given annually to an outstanding high school student in the Kalamazoo Public School system.

Walker is an inventor with several U.S. patents to his credit and, in his spare time, he loves performing magic. He is a 1961 graduate of The Ohio State University with a Master of Arts degree in sociology. He graduated in 1964 with a Ph.D. in the same major. A member of Alpha Kappa Delta Honorary Fraternity, he is also a member of Alpha Phi Alpha Fraternity, Inc. and Phi Kappa Phi.

Walker was married to the late Georgia E. Doles-Walker, and has one granddaughter, Tracy Williams, and one great granddaughter, Cashe Williams.

Douglas L. Williams

Senior Vice President, General Counsel
Limited Brands, Inc.

Class of 1980

Douglas L. Williams joined Limited Brands in December of 1998 and is its senior vice president, general counsel. In this leadership role, he is responsible for the legal affairs for the entire organization. In addition, he is responsible for both the company's regulatory compliance group and the global trade compliance group. These two groups ensure the delivery of quality services as it relates to regulatory compliance, product safety, customs, labor practices and brand protection. He also serves as the chairman of the company's Business Ethics Committee and is co-leader of the company's Values and Inclusion Steering Committee. Limited Brands is the nation's premier specialty retailer, with annual sales of $9.4 billion through approximately 3,100 stores which include Victoria's Secret, Bath & Body Works, La Senza, White Barn Candle Co. and Henri Bendel.

Prior to joining The Limited, Williams was a partner with the Columbus, Ohio, based law firm of Vorys, Sater, Seymour and Pease, LLP. From 1985-1993, he was a partner with the law firm of Schwartz, Kelm, Warren & Rubenstein.

Williams was an assistant professor of law at The Ohio State University from 1984 to 1985 where he taught employment discrimination law and labor law. He was also an adjunct professor of law at The Ohio State University teaching employment law litigation. Williams has been an active speaker and author for various groups throughout the country. He is on the board of the Center for Child and Family Advocacy, the Community Shelter Board and formerly served on the Franklin County United Way board of trustees as the chair of the United Way Safety Vision Council.

Williams is a member of the Ohio and California bars. He received a Bachelor of Science degree from the U.S. Air Force Academy, a Master of Science degree from Central Missouri State University, and a juris doctorate degree (with honors) from The Ohio State University. He is a member of the Order of The Coif and was on The Ohio State Law Review while attending The Ohio State University College of Law.

Williams and his children reside in Columbus, Ohio.

Robert L. Wright Jr., O.D.
Chairman & Chief Executive Officer
FE Holdings, Inc.

Class of 1960

A native of Columbus, Georgia, Dr. Robert L. Wright received a Bachelor of Science degree in optometry from the College of Optometry at The Ohio State University. With more than 50 years of experience in government, business, finance, and project management, he also served three consecutive terms as a member of the Columbus, Georgia City Council. Wright was appointed by President Reagan to the position of associate administrator for Minority Small Business at the Small Business Administration.

Starting with only three employees in 1985, Wright built Dimensions International into a world-class organization with more than 100 offices in ten countries and more than 1,500 employees in 16 different time zones. He served as chairman and CEO, and later chairman emeritus and senior advisor until 2007 when the company was sold to Honeywell for $230 million. Later, he served as chairman of Flight Explorer (FE), which he purchased from DI prior to the sale of DI to Honeywell. FE is a global flight tracking, information technology and communications solutions provider to the business aviation and traveler community. He sold FE to Sabre Technologies and became chairman and CEO of FE Holdings, Inc., a company dedicated to the entrepreneurial spirit of investment and growth in the private and development sectors with interests in motorsports, gaming, entertainment, real estate and lighting.

Wright serves on several boards including Aflac, the Horatio Alger Association, The Ohio State University Capital Campaign Steering Committee, The Ohio State University Foundation, and is vice chairman of the board of trustees for Morehouse School of Medicine. He is former chairman of the Presidential Commission for the National Museum of African American History and Culture in Washington, D.C., and a former member of the Ohio State Alumni Advisory Council.

Residing in Columbus, Georgia, Wright has received numerous awards and was recently inducted into the Horatio Alger Association receiving the Horatio Alger Award for Distinguished Americans. He was initiated into Kappa Chapter of the Alpha Phi Alpha Fraternity, Inc. in 1956 at The Ohio State University and served two terms as chapter president.

The Ohio State University Athletics Department-Points of Pride

Overall

- With 36 varsity sports, Ohio State is the largest fully funded athletics program in the country and is a totally self-supporting auxiliary unit of the University.
- During the 2010-11 fiscal year, the Department of Athletics will pay nearly $30 million of its $128 million dollar budget to the University for funding support toward theUniversity's academic mission, including nearly $15 million in grant-in-aid reimbursement.
- *U.S. News and World Report* ranks Ohio State as one of the Top 20 public universities.

The People

- In 2010 Gene Smith, assistant vice president and director of athletics at Ohio State was the recipient of the *Sports Business Journal* Athletics Director of the Year. He also will serve as the 2011 NCAA Men's Basketball Tournament Chair.
- Following the 2009 football season, the Ohio State Department of Athletics received an AT&T National Sportsmanship award from the National Association of Directors of Athletics for its Armed Forces tribute in its home opener vs. Navy Sept. 5.
- Each year, Ohio State student-athletes, coaches and staff members are involved in thousands of hours of community service.
- In 2009-10, the Department of Athletics will transfer its fourth $1 million contribution payment to the University toward its $9 million commitment to fund the Thompson Memorial Library renovation, which reopened August 3, 2009.

The Tradition

- All-time, Ohio State teams have combined for 62 national titles.
- Ohio State has won national championships in baseball, men's basketball, fencing, football, men's golf, men's gymnastics, pistol, men's track, men's swimming and synchronized swimming.
- All-time, there are more than 2,000 Buckeye All-Americans including 85 in 2009-10.
- Buckeyes have won a total of 327 individual national championships with five coming in 2008-09.

The Excellence

- The overall grade point average of the more than 1,000 Ohio State student-athletes is 3.04 with a total of 503 at 3.0 or higher.
- The Buckeyes topped the Big Ten for the seventh consecutive year with a record 346 Academic All-Big Ten selections. Ohio State also led the conference with 67 Distinguished Scholars with GPAs of 3.7 or higher.
- In 2008-09, 28 teams represented Ohio State in postseason play and combined for eight conference championships.
- All-time, Ohio State has won 294 combined conference championships with 195 Big Ten titles.

OSU ATHLETIC DIRECTOR

Gene Smith is in his seventh year as director of athletics at The Ohio State University. He was named to his current position March 5, 2005. On March 17, 2008, Gordon Gee, president of The Ohio State University, promoted Smith to university assistant vice president/director of athletics and he has since been named associate vice president/director of athletics. Smith is the eighth person to hold the athletics director position at Ohio State and the first African-American to do so. He previously served as director of athletics at Arizona State, Iowa State and Eastern Michigan universities.

At Ohio State, Smith oversees the nation's most comprehensive and most successful college athletic programs. The Buckeyes have 36 fully-funded varsity sports and more than 1,000 student-athletes. The department of athletics is completely self supporting and receives no university funds, tax dollars or student fees. In fiscal year 2009-10, the department transferred nearly $30 million in assessments to the university, including more than $13 million in grant-in-aid reimbursement. In Smith's first three years at Ohio State, the department of athletics finished in the black financially and increased its reserve fund.

Upon arriving at Ohio State, Smith quickly established himself as a respected and thoughtful leader, both within the university and the community. In the spring of 2007, he unveiled a five-year strategic plan, reflecting the department's goals and values. The strategic planning process, inclusive of the entire department, emphasized the development of the total student-athlete.

Gene Smith
Associate Vice President/Director of Athletics
The Ohio State University

Under Smith's leadership, The Ohio State Department of Athletics was honored in the spring of 2008 with the Diversity in Athletics Award in the category of Overall Excellence in Diversity. Smith accepted the honor at the 43rd annual National Association of College Directors of Athletics Convention in Dallas. Shortly after Ohio State was honored as a department for its dedication to diversity, Smith was individually recognized for his contribution to the sport of football.

The National Football Foundation & College Hall of Fame, announced in June of 2008 the recipients of the NFF's 2008 Major Awards. Smith was honored officially December 9, 2008, in New York with the John L. Toner Award. Presented annually, the Toner Award is given to a director of athletics who has demonstrated superior administrative abilities and shown outstanding dedication to college athletics and particularly college football.

Smith recently was appointed to the Governing Board of Trustees of the Lincoln Theatre Association. He was named to the position by the Franklin County (Ohio) Board of Commissioners. It is a three-year appointment effective March 10, 2009.

Smith has an exemplary record of national leadership and service. In 2007, he served as president of the Division 1-A Athletic Directors Association.

He is entering his seventh year on the prestigious NCAA Men's Basketball Committee and was appointed chair of the committee for the 2010-11 academic year, with his term as chair beginning September 1, 2010. Smith served on the Basketball Academic Enhancement Group, a 27-member panel charged with developing strategies to enhance academic performance and graduation rates in Division I men's basketball.

Smith is past president of the National Association of Collegiate Directors of Athletics (NACDA) and was that organization's first African-American president. He has also served on the NCAA Management Council, the NCAA Committee on Infractions, the NCAA Executive Committee, the NCAA Football Rules Committee, the President's Commission Liaison Committee, the NCAA Baseball Academic Enhancement Task Force and the National Football Foundation Honors Court, among others.

In recognition of his service, Smith was named by *Black Enterprise* magazine as one of the 50 Most Powerful African Americans in College Sports. In 2007 he was named to NACDA's inaugural "Legends Class," and was also named Athletic Administrator of the Year by the Black Coaches Association (BCA). In 2002-03, he received NACDA's AD of the Year honors for the Division 1-A West Region.

In May of 2010 Smith was honored as the *Sports Business Journal* Athletic Director of the Year. The award, for which he was a finalist in 2008, was based on excellence and outstanding achievement in the business of sports for the period of January 1, 2009-February 28, 2010.

Smith grew up in Cleveland, Ohio, and attended the University of Notre Dame on a football scholarship. He played four years of football as a defensive end for the Irish and was a member of the 1973 Associated Press national championship team. Smith received his bachelor's degree in business administration from Notre Dame in 1977. Following graduation, he joined the Notre Dame coaching staff under Dan Devine and remained in that capacity until 1981. The 1977 Notre Dame team captured the undisputed national championship.

Smith left Notre Dame following the 1981 season to accept a marketing position with IBM. He returned to college athletics in April of 1983 as assistant athletic director at Eastern Michigan University. In 1985, he was appointed as interim director of athletics at Eastern, a position he held until 1986 when he became the director on a full-time basis. In 1993, Smith was named director of athletics at Iowa State University. He moved to Arizona State as director of athletics in 2000.

As a former college athlete and coach, Smith is passionate about the well being of student-athlete. "We want to create an environment for our student-athletes to be successful academically, athletically and socially," he says. "The student-athlete experience provides teachable moments that prepare young women and men for success in life."

Smith is active in the Columbus community and is a member of the board of the YMCA of Central Ohio and the Boys and Girls Club of Greater Columbus. He also is active with the Bell Center for African-American males on Ohio State's campus.

Gene and his wife, Sheila, have four children, Matt, Nicole, Lindsey and Summer, and two grandchildren, Marshall and Steele. Sheila, a 1976 Canadian Olympian in basketball, holds a doctorate degree in higher education administration and is an associate vice president for development at Ohio State.

Courtesy, OhioStateBuckeyes.com

Go Buckeyes!

Dwight Hudson
Drum Major 1977-1979

Fred D. Patterson (top row, third from left) - In 1889 Fred was the first African-American student enrolled at Ohio State. Additionally, he was also the first OSU varsity football player. He played on the 1891, 1892 and 1893 teams.

WILLIAM "BILL" WILLIS

OCTOBER 2, 1921 – NOVEMBER 27, 2007

By Jessica A. Johnson, Ph.D. 

When the Cleveland Browns became a charter member of the All-America Football Conference (AAFC) in 1946, a dynasty was born and a racial barrier was broken. Bill Willis, a talented and lightening quick guard from Ohio State became one of the trailblazers to break the unofficial ban on blacks in professional football that had been established in 1933. Before trying out for the Browns, Willis was head football coach and athletic director at Kentucky State College. Although he was fulfilling his career goals as a coach and administrator, Willis yearned to play pro ball.

Bill Willis, 1942

William "Bill" Willis

He reasoned that with a few years of experience at the professional level he would be a better college coach. When Willis found out that Paul Brown, his former OSU coach, was taking the helm in Cleveland in the newly formed AAFC, Willis called and asked for an opportunity to make the team.

Brown was keenly aware of Willis' athletic ability since Willis had been a star lineman for the Buckeyes. Willis entered OSU in 1941 and expected to star in track and field. He was considered small for a lineman, barely weighing over 200 pounds, but Brown was impressed with Willis' speed. Willis earned a starting position his sophomore year and helped lead Ohio State to the Big Ten conference title and national championship in 1942. Willis went on to receive All American honors in 1943 and 1944.

Due to the ban on African Americans in the pros, becoming a professional football player seemed unlikely for Willis.

However, when Willis asked Brown for an opportunity to try out in Cleveland, Brown noticed that there was nothing specific in the charter of the AAFC that prevented blacks from playing in the league. Willis was signed to a $4,000 contract and the Browns then added Marion Motley, a standout African-American fullback, to the team. Willis and Motley broke professional football's color barrier a year before Jackie Robinson made his Brooklyn Dodgers debut.

Willis became the nucleus of the Browns' defensive unit that was number one against scoring during their four years in the AAFC. Playing middle guard, he continued to wreak havoc on offensive linemen who were not able to handle his speed after the ball was snapped. Willis' quickness in reacting to the ball earned him the nickname "The Cat," and football historians credit him for fashioning what is presently known as the middle linebacker position. When the AAFC dissolved in 1949, the Browns joined the NFL during the 1950 season. Willis played three more years in Cleveland and then retired to become the city's assistant recreation director. He spent the majority of his post-football career working with at-risk youth and became director of Ohio's Youth Commission in 1963.

As a result of his outstanding efforts, William Willis High School in Powell, Ohio, was established in his honor.

Willis was inducted into the College Football Hall of Fame in 1971 and the Pro Football Hall of Fame in 1977. He continued to share his life lessons from the gridiron with young people until his death at age 86 in 2007. Willis always stressed to youth that character was most important, and he truly exemplified this standard on and off the field.

O-H

I-O

Dick Delaney

Former Associate Athletic Director

Dick Delaney made an impact during his 15 years with The Ohio State University Athletic Department. He joined Ohio State staff in 1970 as assistant director of athletics, the university's first African-American athletic administrator. He was named associate director in 1977.

His chief responsibilities were to conduct special programs, especially the National Youth Sports Program (NYSP) and Buckeye Summer Sports Camps. He served as supervisor of the ice rink, coordinator of the work-study program, administered the book loan program, coordinated team travel and was advisor to the cheerleading squad.

Delaney came to Ohio State with a rich background in the operation of youth recreation and settlement programs. He conducted programs in Akron, Chicago and Cleveland before joining the Ohio State staff.

A native of Akron, Ohio, Delaney was a 1954 graduate of Western Reserve University. As an undergraduate, he played football and basketball.

He was inducted into the Case Western Reserve University Athletic Hall of Fame in 1980. Returning to Case Western Reserve in 1969, Delaney served as an assistant football coach for two years and was head basketball coach for one season. He earned a master's degree in 1970.

Delaney was a life member of Kappa Alpha Psi, a member of the development fund board at Children's Hospital and a veteran of the Korean War.

He and his wife, Bee, had two sons, both Ohio State graduates and members of the football team. Keenan ('84) was a student manager and Kevin ('86) was a walk-on, who earned a scholarship as a wide receiver and running back.

Delaney died on February 11, 1985, following a two-year battle with cancer. He was a man who was admired and respected by all those who had the privilege to know and work with him.

The Ohio State University cheerleaders pyramid, 1972

William "Bill" Myles

Assistant Football Coach
Associate Athletic Director

William "Bill" Myles
Assistant Football Coach 1977-1984
Associate Athletic Director 1985-2007

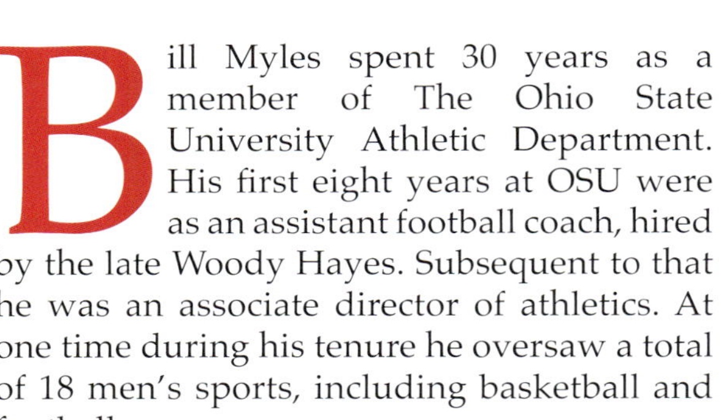

Bill Myles spent 30 years as a member of The Ohio State University Athletic Department. His first eight years at OSU were as an assistant football coach, hired by the late Woody Hayes. Subsequent to that he was an associate director of athletics. At one time during his tenure he oversaw a total of 18 men's sports, including basketball and football.

Myles joined the OSU Staff in 1977; he remained in coaching until 1985 and was considered one of the top offensive line tutors in college football during his stay with the Buckeyes. Prior to that, he was an assistant football coach at the University of Nebraska, Lincoln from 1972 to 1977.

Myles is a native of Kansas City, Missouri, and a graduate of Drake University. He earned a Master of Arts degree from Central Missouri State, awarded in 1967.

To his credit, he coached in 13 bowl games during his 13-year coaching career including the Rose, Orange, Sugar, Cotton, Gator and Fiesta Bowls. He is the recipient of his alma mater's two most prestigious awards, the Double D Award (for athletics and service) and the Distinguished Alumni Service Award. In 1972 he was awarded High School Coach of the Year at Southeast High School in Kansas City.

Previously, he was a member of the Fellowship of Christian Athletes.

Bill and his wife, Lorita, have two adult children, Debbie (OSU '80) and Bill, and two grandchildren, Markus and Kennedi.

Terrelle Pryor

Jim Parker

Played as guard for OSU from 1954-56. Played on the 1954 national championship team, named All-American in 1956 and won the Outland Trophy. Inducted into the College Football Hall of Fame in 1974.

Arnold Birtho

Lettered for OSU in 1957-59. In those seasons OSU was 9-1 ; 1957 co-national title.

Aurealius Thomas

All-American guard for OSU from 1955-1957. Played on 1957 national championship team.

Jim Marshall

All-American at tackle for OSU in 1958. Played in the NFL for one season with the Cleveland Browns and 19 with the Minnesota Vikings.

Bob Ferguson

Running back and member of College Football Hall of Fame 1996. All-American in 1960-61. In 2000 he was selected to the Ohio State Football All-Century team. 1st round NFL draft pick of Pittsburgh Steelers.

Paul Warfield

Named All-Big Ten in 1962 and '63. Played on the national championship team and went on to become one of the NFL's greatest receivers, playing eight seasons with the Cleveland Browns and five with Miami Dolphins. Inducted to the Pro Football Hall of Fame in 1983.

John Brockington

Halfback and fullback for OSU from 1968-70. Led Buckeyes to undefeated season and national championship in 1968. Drafted into NFL as 1st round pick of Green Bay Packers. NFL Rookie of the Year in 1971.

John Hicks

Three-year letterman at OSU; All-Big Ten and All-American selection and winner of the Lombardi Award and the Outland Trophy. Enshrined In the College Football Hall of Fame in 2001. Played with NY Giants and the Pittsburgh Steelers.

Orlando Pace

Coach Rudy Hubbard with players, 1970

Brian Baschnagel, Cornelius Greene, Pete Johnson, Archie Griffin

Jack Tatum

BILLY HILL

OHIO STATE UNIVERSITY ATHLETIC TRAINER

Billy Hill was a member of The Ohio State University's Department of Athletics staff from 1971 to 1995, serving as head athletic trainer for football from 1974 until his untimely death in 1995.

Hill had extensive experience in track, serving as head trainer for the United States' track teams at the 1984 Olympics in Los Angeles, the 1975 Pan American Games in Mexico City, and the 1983 World Track and Field Championships in Helsinki. In May of 1993, he was appointed to the U.S. Olympic Committee's Sports Medicine Council and was to have played an integral role in establishing the sports medicine policies for the 1996 Olympics in Atlanta.

A native of Memphis, Tennessee, Hill served three years in the U.S. Army, including a tour of duty as a medical specialist in Vietnam, before enrolling at Ohio State. He graduated in 1973 with a Bachelor of Science degree in education.

Hill served as president of the Ohio Athletics Trainers Association. The organization named Hill University and Collegiate Trainer of the Year in 1988, at which time he was also inducted into The Ohio State University Athletic Hall of Fame. The Ohio State football team played their 1995-96 season in his honor. In 1996 the university also dedicated a Distinguished Service Award in his name.

THE HEISMANS

Eddie George

Archie Griffin

Troy Smith

Cris Carter

Troy Smith

Chris "Beanie" Wells and President E. Gordon Gee

Santonio Holmes, Jack Tatum, Cris Carter and Mike Doss

Mallory E. (Donaldson) Mitchell

Telex
97
90
50
10

BIG TEN CHAMPIONS
VALUE CITY ARENA
Nationwide
OHIO STATE
BUCKEYES

Kroger
cingular
The Ohio State University Medical Center
Huntington Banks
Nationwide
On Your Side
MIRROR LAKE
TOWERS
UNIVERSITY HALL
TOWERS
MIRROR LAKE
cingular
ING
JAMES CANCER HOSPITAL
SOLOVE RESEARCH INSTITUTE
at&t
at&t
OHIO STATE
BUCKEYES

JACKSON
22

Former Head Coach Randy Ayers

Randy Ayers was the men's basketball coach at OSU from the 1989-90 season until 1997. He earned a Big Ten Coach of the Year title and a National Coach of the Year title. He took the team to the 1st seed in the region but never reached the final four.

Mel Nowell

Played as guard for the OSU basketball team that won the 1960 NCAA championship with three Hall of Famers. Played in the NBA for the Chicago Zephyrs and in the ABA.

Kelvin Ransey

Four-year starter at OSU from 1976 to 1979, where he played as point and shooting guard. Was fourth overall pick in the 1980 draft by the Chicago Bulls.

Herb Williams

Four-year starter for OSU men's basketball. Williams is the school leader in career field goals made. He is second all-time in career blocked shots. Was named to the All-Big Ten team as a junior. Played from 1977-1981. Was 1st round draft pick of Indiana Pacers.

Yvette Angel

Point guard for OSU Lady Buckeyes. Led them to four straight Big 10 titles and a Final 8 appearance in the NCAA tournament. Fourth all-time leading scorer in 1985 when she graduated. Honored as All Big-Ten selection for three seasons and as an All-American.

Clark Kellogg

Played for OSU men's basketball team from 1979-82. Earned All-Big Ten Conference and MVP in 1996. 1st round draft pick of Indiana Pacers. Clark is now a CBS Sports Analyst.

Jim Cleamons

As a rookie guard on the legendary 1971-72 Lakers NBA Championship team that won a professional sports record 33 consecutive games, Jim Cleamons served mostly an ancillary role, seeing limited playing time on a team filled with future Hall-of-Famers. However, upon his return to Los Angeles 28 years later, Cleamons' impact has been much more profound, serving as an assistant coach and helping guide the Lakers to five championships in 2000, 2001, 2002, 2009 and 2010.

Tracy Hall

Jessica Davenport

Lawrence Funderburke

Granville Waiters

Jim Jackson

Dennis Hopson and Tracy Hall

2007 Big Ten Women's Basketball Championship Team

2007 Big Ten Men's Basketball Championship Team

Jared Sullinger

James "JJ" Sullinger

Evan Turner

David Lighty

Michael Redd

Greg Oden

BIG TEN CHAMPIONS
DSW SHOES
VALUE CITY ARENA
OHIO

NATIONAL CHAMPIONS
1960
BIG LOTS!
M/I HOMES
AAA

Butch Reynolds Olympic gold and sliver medalist.

Stephanie Hightower

OHIO STATE

OHIO STATE
OHIO STATE
OHIO STATE

OHIO

Head Coach Miles Avery

Since taking command of the men's gymnastics program in 1998, head coach Miles Avery is a four-time U.S. Olympic assistant coach, who has led Ohio State to one NCAA title and five Big Ten championship crowns, including a program record three-consecutive conference titles in 2005, '06 and '07.

OTHER NOTABLE ALUMNI

Some notable accomplishments and achievements gained by African-American students and alumni at The Ohio State University include:

Abraham L. Davis (Ph.D., Political Science, 1969) joined the political science faculty at Morehouse College in the late 1960s, serving twice as department chair. He has authored numerous books, including *The Supreme Court, Race and Civil Rights*, the landmark text on the Supreme Court's role in civil rights, which is used in undergraduate classrooms throughout the country. Davis retired from Morehouse College in 2008 and currently serves as a consultant with the U. S. State Department.

Helen G. Edmonds (M.A. and Ph.D., History) was one of the first African-American woman to earn a doctoral degree from The Ohio State University. She also became the first African-American woman in the United States to serve as dean of a graduate school (North Carolina Central University.)

Ruby Elzy (1930) was a singer and actress. She played the role of Serena in *Porgy and Bess* more than 800 times. She sang on the radio with Bing Crosby and at the White House for Eleanor Roosevelt. Elzy came to The Ohio State University from Mississippi to study voice under Royal D. Hughes, founder and director of the university's music department. Elzy died in 1943 at the age of 35.

Charles W. Gray (B.A., Political Science) graduated from The Ohio State University in 1950 from the College of Arts & Sciences. He was a distinguished and lifelong member of Kappa Alpha Psi Fraternity, Zeta Chapter. He worked for the U.S. Postal Service for 35 years and retired in 1989. Gray cherished being a Buckeye and passed on the importance of education and love of Buckeye sports to all his friends and family members.

Rada Higgins McCreadie (Ph.D., Mathematics) Dr. Higgins received her Ph.D. from The Ohio State University. She has publications in *Elemente der Mathematik*, *Canadian Mathematical Bulletin*, and the *Fibonacci Quarterly* is cited in the *Encyclopedia of Mathematics*, 1987. Higgins says her favorite problem is one she solved years ago: a proof of the generalized Pythagorean Equation on the basis of principles dating from the Egyptian papyri, dating from 1800 B.C.

John B. Williams (B.A. Fine Arts, 1950), a native of Columbus, Ohio served in World War II as part of the legendary Buffalo Soldiers, WWII's first African-American infantry combat unit in Europe. After the war, Williams returned to Columbus and worked for the U.S. Postal Service for 39 years.

Dale R. Wright (B.A., College of Journalism, 1950), noted African-American journalist, author and Pulitzer Prize nominee, died in December of 2009. Wright was the first African American inducted into Ohio State's chapter of Sigma Delta Chi, a national journalism fraternity. Wright enrolled in The Ohio State University's School of Journalism in the late 1940s and served as the news editor of the student newspaper, *The Lantern*. Wright was the first reporter to integrate the newsroom of the old Scripps Howard paper, the *New York World-Telegram and Sun*.

A SPECIAL THANKS TO THESE OSU SUPPORTERS

Hal Keller
President
Jack Kukura
Chief of Acquisitions
Ohio Capital For Housing, OCCH
88 East Broad Street, Suite 1800
Columbus, OH 43215
614.224.8446

Dr. Robert Polite
Integrative & Lifestyle Medicine
The Polite Care
Mount Carmel Cherry Way Center
1329 Cherry Way Drive, Suite 700
Gahanna, OH 43230
Phone: 614.476.CARE
www.ThePoliteCare.com

Luther M. Henson
Senior Sales Associate
Miracle Motor Mart
OSU Varsity "O" Alumni, New England Patriot
2380 Morse Rd.
Columbus, OH 43229
Cell: 614.746.3248
Email: luther@miraclemotormart.com

Carl D. Smallwood
Partner, Attorney at Law
Vorys, Sater, Seymour and Pease, LLP
52 East Gay Street
Columbus, OH 43215
Phone: 614.464.6400
www.vorys.com

BIOGRAPHICAL INDEX

BIOGRAPHICAL INDEX

Sponsors' Index